Foundations of Syntactic Theory

PRENTICE-HALL FOUNDATIONS OF MODERN LINGUISTICS SERIES

Sanford A. Schane

editor

John P. Kimball The Formal Theory of Grammar

Robert P. Stockwell Foundations of Syntactic Theory

Robert P. Stockwell, Dale E. Elliott, and Marian C. Bean Workbook in Syntactic Theory and Analysis

Sanford A. Schane Generative Phonology

George L. Dillon Introduction to Contemporary Linguistic Semantics

Maurice Gross Mathematical Models in Linguistics

Suzette Haden Elgin What Is Linguistics?

Other titles to be announced

Foundations
of
Syntactic
Theory

ROBERT P. STOCKWELL

University of California, Los Angeles

PRENTICE-HALL, INC., Englewood Cliffs, New Jersey

Library of Congress Cataloging in Publication Data

STOCKWELL, ROBERT P
  Foundations of syntactic theory.

  (Prentice-Hall foundations of modern linguistics series)
  Bibliography: p.
  Includes index.
  1. Grammar, Comparative and general—Syntax.
2. Generative grammar. I. Title.
P291. S68   415   76-8021
ISBN 0-13-329987-2
ISBN 0-13-329979-1 pbk.

Printed in the United States of America

10 9 8 7 6 5 4 3 2 1

PRENTICE-HALL INTERNATIONAL, INC., LONDON
PRENTICE-HALL OF AUSTRALIA PTY. LTD., SYDNEY
PRENTICE-HALL OF CANADA, LTD., TORONTO
PRENTICE-HALL OF INDIA PRIVATE LIMITED, NEW DELHI
PRENTICE-HALL OF JAPAN, INC., TOKYO
PRENTICE-HALL OF SOUTHEAST ASIA PTE. LTD., SINGAPORE

To Archibald Anderson Hill:

Gentleman, Scholar, Teacher, and Good Friend

Editor's Note

Language permeates human interaction, culture, behavior, and thought. The *Foundations of Modern Linguistics Series* focuses on current research in the nature of language.

Linguistics as a discipline has undergone radical change within the last decade. Questions raised by today's linguists are not necessarily those asked previously by traditional grammarians or by structural linguists. Most of the available introductory texts on linguistics, having been published several years ago, cannot be expected to portray the colorful contemporary scene. Nor is there a recent book surveying the spectrum of modern linguistic research, probably because the field is still moving too fast, and no one author can hope to capture the diverse moods reflected in the various areas of linguistic inquiry. But it does not seem unreasonable now to ask individual specialists to provide a picture of how they view their own particular field of interest. With the *Foundations of Modern Linguistics Series* we will attempt to organize the kaleidoscopic present-day scene. Teachers in search of up-to-date materials can choose individual volumes of the series for courses in linguistics and in the nature of language.

If linguistics is no longer what it was ten years ago, its relation to other disciplines has also changed. Language is peculiarly human and it is found deep inside the mind. Consequently, the problems of modern linguistics are equally of concern to anthropology, sociology, psychology, and philosopy. Linguistics has always had a close affiliation with literature and with foreign language learning. Developments in other areas have had their impact on linguistics. There are mathematical models of language and formalisms of its structure. Computers are being used to test grammars. Other sophisticated instrumentation has revolutionized research in phonetics. Advances in neurology have contributed to our understanding of language pathologies and to the development of language. This series is also intended, then, to acquaint other disciplines with the progress going on in linguistics.

Finally, we return to our first statement. Language permeates our lives. We sincerely hope that the *Foundations of Modern Linguistics Series* will be of interest to anyone wanting to know what language is and how it affects us.

Sanford A. Schane, *editor*

Contents

Syntactic Categories   34

Surface Syntactic Information   63

Constituent Structure   86

Types of Syntactic Rules   114

Communicative Functions of Syntactic Rules   144

Preface

In reflecting on the huge literature that concerns the syntax of natural languages, one is hard-pressed to find explanations that are satisfying, that feel fundamental, that seem to get down to some sort of noncircular bedrock. One is not at all pressed to find examples of new and intricate esoteric academic games, as though the task of scholarship were to invent, and reinvent, new rules for chess or bridge at regular intervals. It is indeed hard to believe, when you examine these inventions dispassionately, that they can be wholly serious, not tongue-in-cheek pastimes, outlets for excessive ingenuity. The inventors of course develop a jargon impenetrable by the nonspecialist, so they are immune to external evaluation: THAT merely defines the field as one of the social sciences, though some other academic genres may also qualify.

It is my belief that language is really simpler than any linguistic theory comes close to suggesting, so that in this book I de-emphasize the detailed formalisms that are part of the various competing theories of syntax and semantics. I cannot see that they lead anywhere. They have to be understood, up to a point, because we can't read the available literature if we don't understand them. I hope the time will come when we won't need to understand such formalisms except as part of the history of linguistics, because what fruit resides in them will have been plucked and stated in readable English, as part of some simpler and more explanatory theory of language than any we have now. An inadequacy of this book (one that worries me; no doubt there are many others that I should also worry about) resides in its failure to provide that simpler theory. Lacking the crucial insight, I have settled for a simpliFIED version of some existing theories, glossing over their game-playing aspects and trying to find a solid kernel of what matters, as I see it, for a beginner to grasp of the fundamental elements—which is what I mean by 'foundations'—of syntax.

The invention and enrichment of language is surely man's most remarkable achievement, and I view the task of characterizing this achievement as one that should be approached seriously and with dignity. But the task cannot be accomplished by inventing precise mathematical formulations of matters where the facts are perceived only hazily. Much of current syntactic theory consists of hazy facts formulated in precise mazes. One can thread his way through jungles of rules to find an insight into a regularity that remains unexplained after all; or, to the extent that it is explained, the explanation could have been reached without torture along the way. I have tried to cut through to the essential elementary facts that any theory must explain; and to eliminate from theories the irrelevant pseudo-precision that frosts over the few insights they provide.

I have no doubt that I have been generous in leaving plenty of matters that need further explication by the instructor or that are open to considerable argument or that need richer exemplification from a wider variety of languages: surely the fun is taken out of the classroom by texts that do everything by themselves. The book is only a beginning. There is a separate book of questions and problems (*Workbook in Syntactic Theory and Analysis*, Stockwell, Elliott, and Bean, Prentice-Hall, 1977) intended both to expand the coverage of this text and to give the reader a chance to dirty his hands with the data of syntax.

I have provided detailed acknowledgments at the end, along with some suggestions about further reading. With these, I hope the reader can himself repair the deficiences of my simplified presentation, if I have succeeded in arousing his curiosity. Three anonymous reviewers have read and commented on my manuscript, to its considerable benefit; and the general editor of this series has been most helpful. Except for their comments at a late state of production, the book was written without feedback from friends or colleagues. I therefore forego the formality of *mea culpa* for what's wrong, since there is no one else on whom I can blame it.

Finally, I want to thank my wife Lucy, whose years of experience as editorial assistant to William Bright on *Language* have provided her with exactly the wrong background for editing and typing an elementary text instead of Sanskrit, Chinese, Proto-Algonkian, and high-flown theory. She has nevertheless struggled manfully—I mean womanfully—with my scribbling, accusing me of male chauvinism on every third example.

R. P. S.

Foundations of Syntactic Theory

Orientation and Aims

To study syntax is to study various aspects of how sentences are formed and how they are understood (i.e., interpreted semantically) in particular languages and in language generally. No language allows sentences to be formed by stringing words together randomly. There are observable regularities. Such regularities may be stated as **rules**, though the word *rule* should not be misunderstood. *Rule* suggests some sort of imperative; in its most familiar sense, a rule is thought of as governing what one SHOULD do. That is NOT the sense in which the word is used here or by most modern grammarians and linguists, though it has indeed been used in precisely this sense by some grammarians and lexicographers who take it as their responsibility to legislate 'correct usage' in the community. Rather, it is understood here to be a GENERALIZATION about regularities observed in the linguistic behavior of speakers of a particular language, and, wherever possible, about such regularities, to the extent that they exist, in ALL languages.

When presented with a syntactic rule about sentence formation in their native language, people are likely to feel that they are being told the obvious: they find it hard to see what is being explained. When told that a rule—say, for example, the rule of subject–verb agreement in English—blocks the formation of ungrammatical sentences[1] like

> *The joggers runs two miles every morning.
>   cf. The joggers run ...
>
> *The boy are leaving at one o'clock.
>   cf. The boy is leaving ...

they feel that you must be joking, that everyone knows you can't say such things: why should you bother to formulate a rule to that effect? If you suggest a more subtle problem—e.g., ask why contraction of auxiliary verbs is not permitted in sentences like

> *I don't know where Bill's.
>   cf. I don't know where Bill is.
>
> *I wonder what time the concert's.
>   cf. I wonder what time the concert is.

people will often jump to the conclusion that contraction is impossible at the end of sentences. But then you note ungrammatical sentences like

> *I wonder what time the concert's tomorrow.
>   cf. I wonder what time the concert is tomorrow.
>
> *I told him what a nice boy you're now.
>   cf. I told him what a nice boy you are now.

and someone is likely to suggest that the impossibility of contraction in such sentences has to do with the importance of the auxiliary in those particular instances, such that it's somehow wrong to downgrade the auxiliary by contracting it.

An adequate explanation of these curious facts, as we shall see much

---

[1] The asterisk (*) is used here and in other works on syntax to mark strings of words that an author believes most native speakers would judge to be ill-formed or unacceptable in respect to some aspect of the grammatical structure that has to be assumed in order to interpret the string of words as a sentence in English (or in whatever language is under discussion). Examples marked by asterisks are made up to illustrate a point about syntax. There is no suggestion intended that such examples reflect an 'error' that some English speaker might actually make. On the contrary, the ungrammatical examples that are generally cited by linguists are often interesting precisely because they COULD NOT occur without the speaker having lapsed from normal behavior in a rather startling and unusual way. WHY can they not occur? What is it, precisely, that is 'strange' or 'impossible' about them? How can this 'strangeness' be characterized in a grammar?

later, can be formulated best in terms of abstract and, from the point of view of any nonlinguist, quite esoteric rules which move parts of the sentence around to different positions. Yet people who speak English do know and understand these rules tacitly, in the sense that they obey them more or less infallibly. If they fail to obey them—i.e., if they should by error come out with one of the ungrammatical sentences—they know that they have made an error and they generally correct it then and there. Superficially, this appears to be a circular argument: if rules are generalizations about regularities in observed behavior, then it is not surprising that the rules turn out to be followed, since if they were not followed, it could only mean that the observations were wrong in the first place.

But the circularity is only superficial. It is indeed circular to claim that rules are followed in the specific set of observations on which they were based, because the rules are merely a convenient abridgment, a compact representation, of that set of observations. If they summarized only the data, they would not be of great interest. They are interesting, and noncircular, only because they also PREDICT THE FORM OF SENTENCES THAT HAVE NOT BEEN OBSERVED. In this sense, they GOVERN the linguistic behavior of speakers. This does not mean that the rules of a language never change: in fact, they are in a constant state of flux. But the flux is not rapid, and at any point in time it is possible to discern a large core of stable, consistent behavior that may be described as **rule-governed** behavior.

Phrases like 'rule-governed behavior' and 'tacit knowledge of the rules' suggest that syntactic rules are somehow real, that they exist in the mind. From the manifest fact that speakers do indeed know in excruciating detail how to form sentences, how to interpret them, and how to put them to use in appropriate circumstances, the study of the psychological aspects of this knowledge—how it is acquired, how it is stored, how speakers manipulate it—has developed into a major area of empirical investigation, PSYCHOLINGUISTICS. It is to be expected that as psycholinguistic studies make us increasingly knowledgeable about the actual processes of language manipulation which take place within the central nervous systems of human beings, the abstract mathematical models that are provided by general theoretical linguistics will have to be drastically altered.

But at this time, the available grammatical theories are not modeled directly on any sort of neurological processing. They are purely abstract, linked to the reality of behavior in quite indirect ways. Because of this indirect aspect of the linkage between the explanation (i.e., the grammar) and the facts (i.e., the observable behavior), it is common to refer to a grammar as being a model of the **competence** of a speaker of the language. What is meant is that there is a regular and uniform correspondence between what the grammar asserts to be true of the language and what the speaker tacitly knows about his language. For instance, if speakers interpret these sentences as meaning the same thing:

The soldiers ordered that the crowd disperse.
The soldiers ordered the crowd to disperse.

then the grammar must characterize the apparent formal differences between them as failing, somehow, to contribute to distinctness of semantic interpretation. Or if the speaker knows that a sentence is ambiguous in a certain way:

Cats won't eat until they're satisfied.
= They won't begin to eat until after they are satisfied.
= They won't keep on eating until they reach the point of satisfaction.

then the grammar must somehow show that the two meanings are a natural consequence of the way that sentence is described in it.

By claiming that his description is a model only of competence (i.e., of the speaker's tacit knowledge), the linguist can avoid saying anything at all about how anyone actually produces a sentence in his language. He can claim that the description of the actual production of meaningful utterances, the **performance** of speakers, is an altogether different task from that of describing competence; and he may further claim that both tasks can be more effectively undertaken by keeping them separate.

There are many shades of interpretation along the scale from 'competence' to 'performance', and vast latitudes for disagreement among scholars. It does not appear that any really substantive matters depend upon this distinction, except one: if a mathematical model of grammatical structure is taken literally as a neurological processing model, there is sure to be confusion and misunderstanding. But as long as the 'rules', 'generalizations', 'descriptions', and 'explanations' that we formulate are understood as being simply the most efficient generalizations we can discover or invent to explain our observations of regularities in the formation and interpretation of the sentences of a language, we can put aside questions about psychological processing for the purposes of studying syntactic theory.

An observation about language which has been around for a long time and which has become central to developments of syntactic theory in the second half of the twentieth century is that people use language CREATIVELY in a very special sense of the word *creative*. The word is not meant in the sense of artistic creativity or innovative creativity. Rather it is used, in this context, to refer to the obvious fact that people do not in general repeat sentences that they have previously heard. They construct new sentences from scratch. Accidentally they will no doubt form some sentences which have occurred before, somewhere, sometime; but it will be chance convergence upon the same string of words to represent the same proposition. It will not, except when reciting a poem or some other set piece (like greetings), be a deliberate act of memory.

The number of possible sentences that anyone can construct is indefinitely large; there is no limit imposed by the grammar of the language. There are limits imposed by time, energy, motivation, and other nonlinguistic capacities of speakers, all irrelevant to the fact that the grammar of a language must be so conceived as to pose no such limitations itself. Nor can the grammar fix a limit on the length of sentences. It is possible to extend a sentence's length indefinitely far by adding on parallel phrases or clauses with conjunctions:

John got tired.
. . . . and went home.
. . . . and watched television . . .

Or various kinds of subordinate phrases or clauses can be attached:

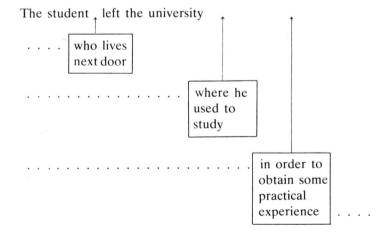

Given any sentence, of any length, one can always make it longer with such devices (given also time enough and life). The grammar must therefore be open-ended in the sense that it specifies no longest sentence and no maximum number of possible sentences. At the same time it must be itself a limited system capable of being mastered in a relatively short time span, since children become fluent and accurate speakers by a fairly early age. A problem that linguists have taken to be crucial is how to capture this infinite creativity within a finite (and readily learnable) device.

Capacities like open-endedness (creativity) and learnability put certain kinds of limitations on the form of rules that grammarians use to express their generalizations. An entire field of study has developed to deal with the problems that have arisen in attempts to characterize the form of rules that are most appropriate and natural for human languages. One does not want rules to be too general in form, for if they are general enough to describe systems that could not possibly be natural human languages, then they presumably could not be pre-wired into the human nervous system (as some linguists believe must be the case, because of the rapidity and ease with which languages are learned by children).

For instance, if we allowed, as a possible grammatical rule, the negation of an assertion by inverting the order of words in the assertion, like this:

ASSERTION
　　The cat disdains canned tuna.

NEGATION BY INVERSION
　　*Tuna canned disdains cat the.
　　i.e., The cat doesn't disdain canned tuna.
　　　　It is not the case that the cat disdains canned tuna.

then we would expect to find some natural language somewhere that made use of this power to construct SOME type of sentence by simple inversion of some OTHER type of sentence. But no such rule exists in any language, from which we conclude that it is unlikely to be a possible type of rule. (Or we might conclude that its absence represents a merely accidental gap; most linguists believe, however, that it is not accidental.) It would in any case be a remarkably inefficient kind of rule that would, at best, put an intolerable burden on the memory. (Try to repeat the previous sentence backwards.)

On the other hand, though the form of rules cannot be allowed to be too general or to impose unreasonable burdens on memory, they must be able to express whatever generalizations we believe should be made in the grammar; we want them to express just the right types, and to exclude the wrong types. It turns out to be a formidable task to constrain the form of grammars in ways which successfully meet these challenges.[2]

Leaving for now the psychological and formal aspects of grammars,

---

[2] For a careful study of the formal properties of rules, see Kimball (1972) or, more broadly, Wall (1972).

let us consider what other kinds of facts grammarians intend to account for when they write a grammar of a language. In what may be thought of as the hard core of syntax, there are two kinds of questions to which answers are sought: questions about **grammaticalness**, and questions about **meaning**. We now consider in some detail the ramifications of these two types of questions.

Grammaticalness:
The Well-formedness Condition

What is meant by 'grammatical' or 'well-formed'? In clear cases, at least, it is easy to see what is meant. Take almost any sentence and the same sentence in reverse order, like these pairs:

> John left the meeting at two o'clock.
> *O'clock two at meeting the left John.

> Not every string of words is grammatical.
> *Grammatical is words of string every not.

No one has any doubt that the second of each pair, the reversed one, is, for practical purposes, a mere random string of English words. As we have already noted, a grammar must contain devices which will block the formation of sentences by this kind of inversion rule or by many other imaginable rules. We examine below a number of ways in which sentences can fail to be well-formed, and the kinds of rules that linguists have invented for the purpose of characterizing these restrictions.

Formal Agreement (Concord)

Agreement rules are a type of constraint on the form of words occurring together. They require that one form must change to match the form of something else, like matching colors—green with green, blue with blue, gold with gold. Thus whether a verb is singular or plural may depend on whether its subject is singular or plural, as in most European languages. The form of an adjective may depend on whether the word that it modifies (the **head noun**) represents a long thin object or a compact object, as in languages of the Bantu family. The form of a main verb may depend on whether its auxiliary verb is *have* or *be* (*is falling* vs. *has fallen*). The variety of possible agreement (or **concord**) rules is enormous. The result of violating such rules is usually only superficial ungrammaticalness, though it is possible to violate these rules in ways which result also in ambiguity or unintelligibility. Their function is usually redundant, but occasionally they are the only available clue to tell the listener what interpretation is intended:

$$\text{Three assistants} \left\{ \begin{array}{l} \text{are} \\ \text{is} \end{array} \right\} \text{adequate for this project.}$$

In this example, *are* agrees with the plural subject and creates no special problem of interpretation. But *is*, not being superficially in agreement, forces the hearer to place some sensible interpretation on the sentence (or, if he fails, to reject it as a slip or error, which is a type of interpretation). There is in fact a readily available interpretation:

(The use of) three assistants is adequate for this project.

The failure of agreement is the only clue to this interpretation.

Since agreement rules are relatively functionless, violation of them rarely impairs the intended sense or contributes to special interpretations as above. Sometimes a language does not provide absolutely clear rules about agreement, and some sentences may therefore be undecidable in respect to their grammaticality:

$$\text{Is everyone finished with} \left\{ \begin{array}{ll} \text{his drink?} & \text{(a)} \\ \text{their drinks?} & \text{(b)} \end{array} \right.$$

Sentence (a) is what the schools teach, but relaxed normal usage among educated speakers probably prefers (b). Notice that the conflict that produces two usages is between FORMAL agreement in (a) vs. SEMANTIC agreement in (b):

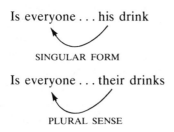

Is everyone . . . his drink

SINGULAR FORM

Is everyone . . . their drinks

PLURAL SENSE

That is, the word *everyone* has the sense of a GROUP of people, so that one expects semantically to refer to the group with some form of PLURAL pronoun (*they, them, their, theirs*). In all areas of grammar, conflicts of this general type exist; syntactic 'rules' are almost never absolute, or exceptionless.

Agreement rules, then, exemplify a class of rules which determine the **form** that words must take if they are to appear together. In all types of constructions where agreement is found, some designated word in the construction controls the form of the other members of the construction. This designated controlling word is called the **head** if the construction is some type of **modifying** one—i.e., one in which all the agreeing words serve to limit more precisely the meaning of the head. Such a headed construction is also called **endocentric**—having its center, or head, within itself.

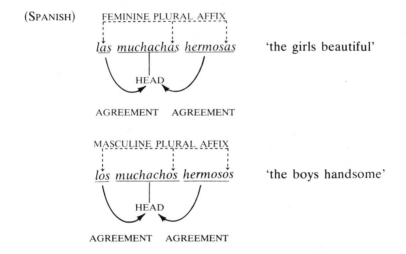

But probably more often in languages of the world, agreeing constructions are not headed; they are **exocentric**, and the function of agreement is to clarify which words are to be construed as part of a single unit, or as having a single referent. Such is the case typically for agreement between subject and predicate, as in the examples cited earlier (*The jogger(s) run(s)* . . .), or between a pronoun and its antecedent, as in *Is everyone finished with his/their drink(s)?*

Agreement rules are simply one of several kinds of devices for specifying that certain forms cannot occur grammatically unless certain other forms also occur in the sentence. Such constraints are therefore called **co-occurrence constraints**—constraints that prohibit or limit forms in respect to the set of linguistic environments in which they can appear.

Some such constraints can be stated, as they are in agreement rules, in terms of the actual surface shape or form of the co-occurring words. Probably more commonly, however, they are stated in terms of whether whole **classes** (or **categories**) of words can be assembled together grammatically. In order to consider examples of such constraints on categorial co-occurrence, we must first clarify some basic notions about sentence structure.

Atomic Sentences

It is linguistically convenient to consider all sentences as belonging to one of two categories: (1) those which are **atomic**, or **basic**, in structure; and (2) those which are in some sense **derived** from atomic sentences. Possibly no two grammarians will make the distinction exactly the same way in every detail, but throughout the history of grammatical studies a distinction has been made which corresponds at least roughly to this one. (Within early versions of the theory of transformational grammar associated with the name of Noam Chomsky—about which much more will be said later—these atomic sentences were called **kernel** sentences.) Our analogy to the composition of matter, implied by the word *atomic*, is revealing. Atoms have an internal structure: they contain a nucleus and satellites, with the weight of the nucleus and number of satellites of an atom of a particular element determining the nature of that element and its place in the periodic table. The variety of stable subatomic structures is strictly limited. However, the atoms themselves may combine to form infinitely varied molecules which are, then, to be analogically understood as derived structures, and they are unlimited in number.

Without pressing the analogy too far, let us consider first the structure of atomic sentences, those simple basic propositions from which larger (molecular) structures can be derived. They are, superficially, made up of sequences of words, but a casual examination of various sequences of words suggests that not just any type of word can occur just anywhere in the sequence. Rather, there must be some word which is understood to express a relation that holds over some domain (the domain in turn expressed by the other words in the sentence). The expression of such a relation is a **predication**. The domain over which the predication is asserted is made up of **participants** (also called **arguments**). Participants are simply names of entities or classes of entities. Their reference—that is, their correspondence to objects in the real world—is determined independently of any particular predicate.

An atomic sentence, then, has a predicate and (with some peculiar exceptions) at least one participant. Participants usually belong to the syntactic class called **nouns** by grammarians, and predicates are typically **verbs** or **adjectives**. The following are atomic sentences in English (ignoring certain matters of mood and tense in the verbs):

PARTICIPANT (NOUN)	PREDICATE (VERB)
John	arrived.
The boy	left.
Those trees	fell down.

The predicates above are called **one-place** predicates, since their domain is only a single participant. In the abbreviated notation of symbolic logic they would be written:

$$P(x) \quad \text{or} \quad (x)P$$

which are completely equivalent; both are read:

$$P \text{ of } x$$

which means:

'The predicate P is asserted of the participant named x.'

Another type of atomic sentence in English involves a **two-place** predicate:

PARTICIPANT (NOUN)	PREDICATE (VERB)	PARTICIPANT (NOUN)
John	loves	Mary.
The boy	left	the room.
Those trees	retain	their leaves.

In abbreviated logical notation, these would be written:

$$P(x, y) \quad \text{or} \quad (x)P(y)$$

which are equivalent, and which mean:

'The predicate P is a relation asserted to hold between two individuals named x and y.'

There is a further bit of crucial information contained in the order, from left to right, in which x and y occur: namely, if the relation is a **transitive** one, then the first participant x is the 'doer' of the action and the second participant y is the one done to. Thus, in $(x)P(y)$, if P is *kill*, then y is the one who gets killed and x is the one who does the killing.

Two atomic sentence structures in English, then, are these:

$(x)P = $ N V   (Noun   Verb)

$(x)P(y) = $ N V N   (Noun   Verb   Noun)

There are others to which we will return. For now it is only necessary to grasp a general notion of what an atomic sentence is like. The notion perhaps can be clarified further by outlining some of the general properties that distinguish atomic from derived sentences in English:

1. Atomic sentences have only one verb:

   N   V
   John arrived at one o'clock.   ATOMIC

   N   V   V
   John arrived to open the conference.   DERIVED

2. Atomic sentences have no words linked by *and, or, but,* or other **conjunctions** that provide for parallel functions:

   N   V
   John arrived at one o'clock.   ATOMIC

   N   CONJ   N   V
   John   *and*   Mary arrived at one o'clock.   DERIVED

   N   V   CONJ   V
   John slept   *and*   ate yesterday.   DERIVED

3. Atomic sentences have only minimal specification of the participants and the predicate (what is meant by 'minimal' can be inferred from the example):

   The⎫ N   V ⎧the⎫   N
       ⎬ cat broke ⎬   ⎨ decanter.   ATOMIC
   A ⎭   ⎩ a ⎭

                N   V   V   N
   My favorite *cat* might possibly *have broken* that gorgeous *decanter* that Aunt Susan gave me.   DERIVED

4. Atomic sentences contain no 'secondary' operators like negation, modality, commanding, questioning:

John left. ATOMIC
John didn't leave. DERIVED
John possibly left. DERIVED
John may have left. DERIVED
Did John leave? DERIVED

Atomic sentences, then, are the simplest affirmative declarative predicational structures of a language. All the others are derived in the sense that they combine atomic sentences in a variety of ways, or they add some specified constant to the sentences (like negation). The following examples are merely to show something of the range of such possible derivations, allowing S to stand for any sentence:

CONJUNCTIONS

S_1 *and* S_2

DISJUNCTIONS

S_1 *or* S_2

CONDITIONS

If S_1, then S_2

MODIFICATIONS (specification of participants)

The boy who S_1 met a girl who S_2

ASSERTIONS OF PROPOSITIONS

John said that S

NEGATIONS OF PROPOSITIONS

John did not leave.
i.e., NOT (John leave)

Given this rough sketch of the notions 'atomic' and 'derived' sentences, it is now possible to examine a type of co-occurrence constraint based not on the form of words, as in agreement rules, but rather on their category membership.

Categorial Co-occurrence

Perhaps the most fundamental difference between predicates stems from the number of participants they allow. This is the distinction already alluded to between one-place, two-place, and three-place (or more) predicates:

ONE-PLACE: $(x)P$

>   John arrived.

$$*\text{John arrived} \left\{ \begin{array}{l} \text{the boy.} \\ \text{the chair.} \\ \text{his friend.} \\ \text{anything.} \\ \cdot \\ \cdot \\ \cdot \end{array} \right\}$$

TWO-PLACE: $(x)P(y)$

$$\left. \begin{array}{l} \text{The boy} \\ \text{John} \\ \text{The rock} \\ \text{Something} \end{array} \right\} \text{hit} \left\{ \begin{array}{l} \text{the door.} \\ \text{Mary.} \\ \text{a car.} \\ \text{something.} \end{array} \right\}$$

>   *John hit.
>   *John needs.
>   *John denied.

THREE-PLACE: $(x)P(y)(z)$

$$\left\{ \begin{array}{l} \text{John} \\ \text{The accident} \end{array} \right\} \text{persuaded} \left\{ \begin{array}{l} \text{Mary} \\ \text{the boy} \\ \text{someone} \end{array} \right\} \{\text{that S}\}.$$

John	gave	Bill	a letter.
*John	gave	Bill.	
*John	gave	a letter.	

But knowing how many participants a predicate allows is not enough. One clearly must also know what kinds of participants are appropriate. This in turn requires subcategorization to answer. Merely asserting that a particular word is a noun and therefore a suitable x or y—i.e., a suitable identification of some individual or class of possible participants—will not suffice to discriminate between predicates over

concrete nouns and predicates over **abstract** nouns (which may themselves be whole sentences):

$$\text{John said} \begin{cases} \text{*the book.} & \text{CONCRETE} \\ \text{that he was tired.} & \text{ABSTRACT} \end{cases}$$

No one knows quite how far such subcategorization has to be carried to eliminate all the sequences that would in fact be judged ungrammatical by speakers of a language. But the degree of detail required is clearly far beyond what has been provided in any existing grammar or dictionary. It is worth a few further examples to try to give the reader a feel for the complexity of such constraints in English. Let us deal briefly with just those categorial constraints that hold between a predicate and the form of a sentence that is embedded (attached) under one of the participants in the structure:

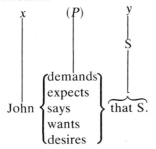

Demand, for instance, requires a subjunctive form of the verb in the lower sentence:

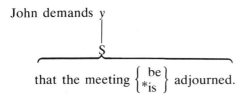

Expect allows the verb of the lower sentence to change to infinitival form, but *demand* does not allow this:

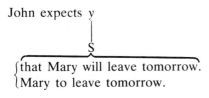

$$\text{John demands} \begin{cases} \text{that Mary leave tomorrow.} \\ \text{*Mary to leave tomorrow.} \end{cases}$$

Say does not allow a subjunctive form of the verb in the lower sentence, but like *demand* it disallows infinitival form in the lower verb:

John says $\begin{cases} \text{that syntax is for the birds.} \\ \text{*syntax to be for the birds.} \end{cases}$

Want, on the other hand, requires this change—the *that*-form is ungrammatical:

John wants $\begin{cases} \text{*that his parents leave him a fortune.} \\ \text{his parents to leave him a fortune.} \end{cases}$

Desire parallels both *want* and *demand,* provided that the verb in the *that*-form is subjunctive:

John desires $\begin{cases} \text{that his wife keep the house cleaner.} \\ \text{*that his wife keeps the house cleaner.} \\ \text{his wife to keep the house cleaner.} \end{cases}$

Inquire disallows all lower sentences of the *that*-type, but accepts lower sentences of other types (*whether*...):

John inquired $\begin{cases} \text{whether she was leaving.} \\ \text{*that she was leaving.} \end{cases}$

Dependency Relations

Agreement rules and categorial constraints share the property of outlawing certain clusterings of words. Essentially they deal with a relation of **dependency**, where the occurrence of one form of a word governs either the form that another word may take or what kind of word or word sequence is possible in the rest of the sentence. It is useful to distinguish between sequences that are bad because they violate universal semantic constraints (i.e., they are bad because they could not conceivably make sense in any language), and sequences that are bad only because the particular language has some arbitrary rules, as all languages do. The former type, those that are universally bad because they can't make sense under any literal interpretation of the meaning of the words, may be illustrated by sentences like the following:

    *The table elapsed.
       cf. Two hours elapsed.
    *She elapsed a week.
       cf. A week elapsed before she returned.
    *He arrived until one o'clock.
       cf. He arrived at one o'clock.
       He didn't arrive until one o'clock.
    *The steel cried uproariously.
       cf. The audience laughed uproariously.

Interpretations may sometimes be deliberately forced onto such apparently nonsensical sequences for serious literary or rhetorical purposes, or in jocular usage: Chomsky's famous example,[3]

    *Golf plays John.
       cf. John plays golf.

gets its effect precisely by forcing one to stretch his imagination to see some sense in which it is possible for golf to play John, e.g., by dominating his every thought and action. Words often acquire new meanings by metaphorical extension into contexts that would be absurd in a literal reading:

    The chairman's proposal won't swing.
    (*swing* extended by analogy to music)
    That idea smells.
    (*smells* = 'is dreadful')
    He's a green doctor.
    (*green* = 'unripened' = 'inexperienced')

On the other hand, the sequences that are bad for arbitrary language-specific reasons are not normally extendable into acceptable metaphorical usage, nor can one usually see any reason why they should be outlawed at all (i.e., the prohibitions do not appear to be motivated by obvious semantic universals):

    *John avoided to look me in the face.
       cf. John avoided looking . . .
    *John heard the music to stop.
       cf. John heard the music stop.
    *On to arrive in Berlin, John began studying German.
       cf. On arriving in Berlin, John . . .
    *He went on Tuesday home.
       cf. He went home on Tuesday.

---

[3] In Chomsky (1961).

Most linguists believe that the problem of excluding sequences that are bad for universal semantic reasons will be solved in some neat way by semantic constraints. To understand better what is meant by 'semantic constraints', consider these examples:

> Horses are animals.
> *Animals are horses.

> Any horse is an animal.
> *Any animal is a horse.

How are the bad examples to be explained? The sentences are **copular** sentences—i.e., two nouns linked by the 'copular' verb *be*. The copula *be* can stipulate three possible kinds of relationship between nouns A and B:

1. A and B refer to the same individual ($A = B$):

   > My favorite pet is that cat.
   > That cat is my favorite pet.

   (Note that both A and B are SPECIFIED EXACTLY, and can occur in either order.)

2. A belongs to the class B ($A \in B$):

   > The professor is a Rotarian.
   > *A Rotarian is the professor.

   (Note that only A is specified exactly—*the professor*—whereas B necessarily refers to any number of individuals.)

3. All members of A are included among the members of B ($A \subset B$):

   > Horses are animals.
   > Any horse is an animal.

   (Note that neither A nor B refers to a specific individual.)

Once we see that our examples are of the third type, namely **class-inclusion**, the explanation of what is bad about

> *Animals are horses.
> *Any animal is a horse.

becomes clear. The intrinsic meaning of *horse* includes the meaning of *animal,* but of course the intrinsic meaning of *animal* does not include the specific attributes of *horse*. Therefore it violates the intrinsic meanings of both words to say,

> *Animals are horses.
> *Any animal is a horse.

It is therefore reasonable to suppose that such a combination would be unacceptable in ANY language, for the same reason, namely that it violates the logical inclusion relationships of the intrinsic meanings of the words.

The distinction between **semantically** ill-formed and **syntactically** ill-formed may be clarified by comparison with another aspect of the structure of language, namely its pronunciation. Neither of these words exists in English:

ftip

stip

But *stip* could be an English word, whereas *ftip* could not be. Since *ftip* could, however, be a word in SOME language, it is a peculiar fact about the rules of English pronunciation, specifically English, that disallows *ftip*. Such rules are like syntactic rules in that they are language-specific. On the other hand, try to imagine a type of pronunciation in which the back of the tongue is expected to articulate against the upper teeth at the front of the mouth. Impossible? Of course—PHYSICALLY impossible. In matters of articulation, physical impossibility is like LOGICAL impossibility in matters of meaning. The parallelism is like this:

```
                       ⎧ violates semantic universals:  MEANINGLESS
              ⎧of words⎨   (logically impossible)
              ⎪        ⎩ violates syntactic constraints:  UNGRAMMATICAL
impossible   ⎨
 sequence    ⎪         ⎧ violates articulatory universals:  UNPRONOUNCEABLE
              ⎩of sounds⎨  (physically impossible)
                        ⎩ violates phonetic constraints:  UNPHONETICAL
```

As it happens, the term 'unphonetical' does not exist, in this sense or any other, but the analogy is clear. Between 'meaningless' and 'ungrammatical' there is a term 'unacceptable' that linguists use to refer to examples that fit the syntactic rules but nevertheless exceed reasonable limitations on human processing capabilities.

Constraints on Movement Rules

Within many formulations of syntactic rules (though not in all), there are some rules which serve to move words or phrases from one position to another within the sentence. The aim of such rules is to show that certain sets of sentences are related to each other in either of two ways:

1. Except for some single semantic constant—some feature like negation or questioning, for example—they are the same in meaning.
2. That part of their meaning known as **cognitive content** is the same (i.e., the conditions are identical under which they would, as isolated statements, be true or false), though they may differ in emphasis, conditions of use, relation to context, or the like.

The problem of stating the conditions under which such **movement rules** result in well-formed sentences is enormously complex and subtle. For instance, these sentences are related (in the first sense above) by the **Interrogative** rule, which moves up to first position some phrase about which information is requested, spells it in a WH-form (like *what, when, where, why*), and attracts the tense or auxiliary to second position:

DECLARATIVE FORM   INTERROGATIVE FORM
The technician erased some tapes.   What tapes did the technician erase?

MOVEMENT:

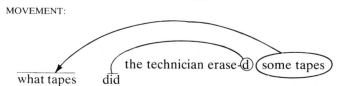

DECLARATIVE   INTERROGATIVE
The chairman will read something.   What will the chairman read?

MOVEMENT:

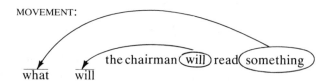

Now suppose that we use the declarative form of these sentences to form a larger sentence (atoms into molecules, to continue the earlier analogy):

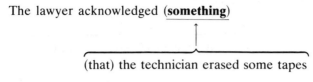

The lawyer acknowledged (**something**)

(that) the technician erased some tapes

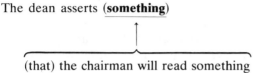

The dean asserts (**something**)

(that) the chairman will read something

It is still possible to extract the same phrases and form questions:

> What tapes did the lawyer acknowledge (that) the technician erased?

> What does the dean assert (that) the chairman will read?

Now we come to the curious fact. If instead of attaching the lower sentence directly to the verb, as above, we instead insert a word like *fact, belief, claim, view, notion* at the front of the lower sentence, it is not then possible to extract any phrase from within the lower sentence and form questions with it in first position:

> The lawyer acknowledged *the fact* that the technician erased some tapes.
> *What tapes did the lawyer acknowledge the fact that the technician erased?

> The dean asserts *his belief* that the chairman will read something.
> *What does the dean assert his belief that the chairman will read?

It is apparent that the constraint makes it impossible to move the questioned word from the lower sentence into the upper one ONLY IF THERE IS AN ADDITIONAL PARTICIPANT AFTER THE HIGHER PREDICATE:

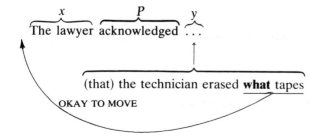

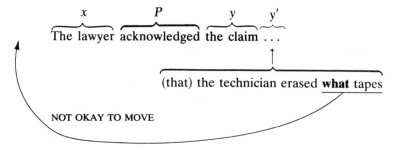

This observation gives a bare clue about the nature of the constraint, though it is beyond the level of this introductory work to pursue the details further here.

Another kind of movement rule, called **Raising**, lifts one of the participants out of a lower sentence and treats it as a participant of the next higher sentence, with certain changes then taking place in the form of the lower one (in particular, the verb becomes infinitival in form):

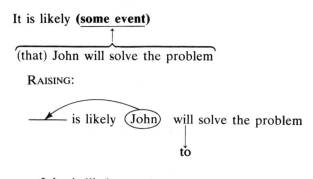

= John is likely to solve the problem.

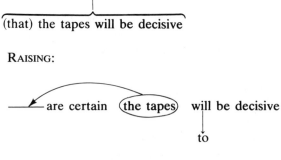

= The tapes are certain to be decisive.

This Raising rule is constrained to a small class of higher predicates. Thus, while Raising is permitted with *likely, certain,* and *sure,* it is impossible with many other semantically similar predicates:

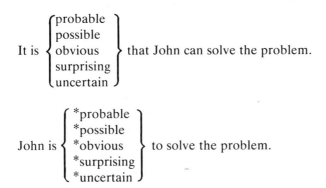

It is ⎧ probable ⎫
⎨ possible ⎬ that John can solve the problem.
⎪ obvious ⎪
⎪ surprising ⎪
⎩ uncertain ⎭

John is ⎧ *probable ⎫
⎨ *possible ⎬ to solve the problem.
⎪ *obvious ⎪
⎪ *surprising ⎪
⎩ *uncertain ⎭

This kind of constraint (limiting the predicates that allow Raising) is different from dependency constraints; the latter merely assert that certain sequences of forms are ungrammatical under ANY conditions. It is also different from constraints on movement rules like the one discussed above that blocks Question-formation if there is a certain type of word between the predicate and the lower sentence from which the questioned word is to be extracted. That constraint depended on the FORM of the sentence. This kind of constraint (on Raising) depends on whether a certain pivotal word—in this case the predicate of the higher sentence— permits the rule to operate. It specifies ungrammaticalness not by virtue of the presence or absence of certain dependent forms, but rather by virtue of the applicability or nonapplicability of certain rules (in this instance a movement rule).

Summary of Conditions on Well-formedness

The great majority of well-formedness constraints belong, then, to one of these two categories:

1. Dependency constraints, of three types:
   a. Form-to-form, as in agreement rules
   b. Category-to-category, as in co-occurrence constraints
   c. Meaning-to-meaning, as in logical inclusion, or in the sense of examples like *The boy elapsed*

2. Constraints on rule application, of two types:
   a. Failure to apply because of the form of the sentence to which an attempted application is made
   b. Failure to apply because of conditions that must be stipulated on some pivotal word in the construction

---

Conditions on Semantic Interpretation:
Hierarchical Structure

We turn now to certain types of conditions on the semantic interpretation of sentences, which define the second major dimension of syntactic theory. It is obvious to anyone who reflects on it that sentences are not understood as some sort of direct left-to-right summation of the meaning of the words in them. Rather the words clot into clusters which then, as units, clot into larger clusters. We therefore say that sentences have **hierarchical** organization. This is most transparently diagramed with boxes inside of boxes, Chinese fashion. Consider the sentence:

Computers are manufacturing tools.

It is ambiguous. It can mean, (1) 'Tools are being manufactured by computers.' Or it can mean, (2) 'Computers are tools for manufacturing.' The difference depends on whether we see the middle two words as a cluster, or the last two:

(1a) Computers $\boxed{\text{are manufacturing}}$ tools.

(2a) Computers are $\boxed{\text{manufacturing tools}}$

After they are boxed one way or the other, they are units ready for further boxing:

(1b) Computers $\boxed{\boxed{\text{are manufacturing}}\ \text{tools}}$

We need to box *tools* with *are manufacturing* because *are manufacturing* is an incomplete predicate which requires a goal, or patient, to which the stated predicate applies. The predicate with its patient serves as the equivalent of an intransitive predicate (as in *Computers have arrived*), and can be boxed with its subject:

(1c) Computers are manufacturing tools

Similarly, we can box *manufacturing tools* together as a unit, and then relate it to the rest of the sentence:

(2b) Computers are manufacturing tools

(2c) Computers are manufacturing tools

Once the idea is clear, we can dispense with the boxes, which are typographically expensive. We can represent the boxes instead with square brackets:

(1a) Computers [are manufacturing] tools

(1b) Computers [[are manufacturing] tools]

(1c) [Computers [[are manufacturing] tools]]

versus

(2a) Computers are [manufacturing tools]

(2b) Computers [are [manufacturing tools]]

(2c) [Computers [are [manufacturing tools]]]

Imagine that each pair of brackets is drawn out to a full box and the iconicity (the relational congruence) of the brackets to the Chinese boxes is apparent.

But it is easy to lose track of which left-hand bracket goes with which right-hand bracket. So most linguists prefer to use tree diagrams in which boxed clusters are tied together by braces:

(1a) Computers are manufacturing tools

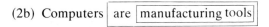

(1b) Computers are manufacturing tools

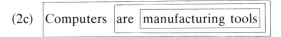

(1c) Computers are manufacturing tools

versus

(2a) Computers are manufacturing tools

(2b) Computers are manufacturing tools

(2c) Computers are manufacturing tools

In order to work with syntactic rules and syntactic structures, it is necessary to become quite proficient in the technique of tree-diagraming. Most linguists are tree-happy, and some even retain a sense of humor about it. The Chicago Linguistic Society published a volume entitled *You Take the High Node and I'll Take the Low Node* ('node' is the top of a brace, the intersection of two lines in a tree-diagram). Fortunately their claim to fame is not limited to their puns.

Conditions on Semantic Interpretation:
Category Labels

It is sufficient, in order to reveal the nature of the ambiguity in *Computers are manufacturing tools,* merely to show the two possible clusterings which force the two distinct semantic interpretations. But for most examples, even of this type, the difference in tree structures—the difference in **bracketing**—is not enough to support a semantic interpretation. It is readily possible to imagine two sequences that are bracketed identically but are still distinct in the relational meanings among the bracketed elements:

John plays basketball

John plays beautifully

The difference lies in the fact that *basketball* is the name of a game, it is something that can be played. It is, in this sentence, a word referring to an entity which serves as a participant in the event represented by the word *plays;* whereas *beautifully,* in the second sentence, is not an entity word at all and cannot ever serve syntactically as a participant in a predication. It is some kind of modifier (and in a deeper analysis it appears to be a predicate, as we shall see). Various paraphrases of these sentences can be construed which make the difference clear:

> John plays basketball.
> = John engages in a certain activity known as *playing* and a particular instances of that activity is known as *playing basketball.*
> = The thing (game) that John plays is basketball.
> = What John plays is basketball.
> = What John does is play basketball.
> ≠ *John's playing is basketball.

> John plays beautifully.
> = John engages in a certain activity known as *playing,* and though we aren't told what kind of playing it is, we are told that it is done in a manner which can be described as beautiful.
> = John's playing is beautiful.
> = What John does is play beautifully.
> = ?How John plays is beautifully. (Okay for some speakers of English.)
> ≠ *What John plays is beautifully.
> ≠ *The thing that John plays is beautifully.

In order to capture more precisely the manner in which we understand these sentences, we can propose SEMANTIC STRUCTURES which are very different from their surface syntactic structures:

PLAY (JOHN, BASKETBALL) = There is a predication of *playing* that holds between two entities, namely John and the game of *basketball.*

$$= P(x, y) \text{ or } (x)P(y)$$

BEAUTIFUL (PLAYING (JOHN'S)) = There is a predication of *beautifulness* that is made about the playing that John does.

$$= B(P(x)) \text{ or } ((x)P)B$$

Put differently: in *John plays beautifully,* there are TWO DISTINCT ONE-PLACE

PREDICATIONS:

1. A certain event is beautiful
2. That event is John's playing

(EVENT) is beautiful

↑

John plays

whereas in *John plays basketball,* there is only ONE TWO-PLACE PREDICA-
TION, namely the predication of *playing-basketball by John.* The tree
structures, looking only at the branches, are identical, but the items that
are bracketed are set up in two different hierarchies.

Now, since it is clear that the two sentences have quite different
semantic interpretations, we must enrich the representation of their
surface structure to show how it is that language users can correctly infer
the appropriate relations. This is the main function of **category labels** in
syntax. Indeed, it is the main function of categorial differences
everywhere in linguistic structure, namely to permit the inference of
different hierarchical semantic relations from linear sequences—i.e., sequences of words that are necessarily linear because they occur in real time,
spoken one after another. We shall examine the details of such category
labels in the next chapter; for now, we merely observe that the CATEGORY
SEQUENCE in

John plays basketball.

is

Noun Verb Noun   (N V N)

which is more or less directly equivalent to

$(x)P(y)$ or $P(x, y)$

where x and y are names of participants in a predication P. But in

John plays beautifully.

the category sequence is

Noun Verb Adverb   (N V ADV)

This sequence is not DIRECTLY equivalent to the semantic formula,

$B(P(x))$ BEAUTIFUL—JOHN'S PLAYING

Instead, it provides the information that *beautifully* is an **adverb**, and then, from what one knows about the nature of adverbs—namely that some of them are **predicates** about some **event**—one can infer the semantic relationships that are symbolized in our formula above. Indeed, the categorization of *beautifully* is probably even more refined than the label 'adverb' suggests: it is a special kind of adverb called a **manner adverb**, and the full interpretation that it imposes on another predicate is something like this:

$$\text{The} \left\{ \begin{array}{l} \text{way} \\ \text{manner} \\ \text{style} \end{array} \right\} \text{—of John's playing—is beautiful.}$$

Conditions on Semantic Interpretation: Paraphrase Relations

Let us turn briefly to other aspects of the way in which syntactic structure relates to meaning. We have considered, so far, two direct relationships between syntax and meaning: hierarchical structure and category labels. The one we shall consider now is an indirect relationship. The two direct relationships discussed have to do with how speakers (and hearers) use syntax in order to assign meanings to even the most basic structures (the atomic sentences of a language). This indirect relationship has nothing to do with the interpretation of atomic sentences but only with the interpretation of complex sentences, those which are formed either by the addition of semantic constants to atomic sentences or by the merger of two or more atomic sentences (with or without additional constants). The relationship is that of **synonymy** or **paraphrase**. 'Synonymy' is ordinarily used to refer to words or phrases which are the same in meaning: *bachelor = unmarried man.* 'Paraphrase' is used to refer to whole sentences which have a certain kind of synonymous equivalence, namely one in which the individual words are kept more or less constant but are switched around in sequence or in hierarchical structure: *It is certain that John will leave = John is certain to leave.* The relationship of synonymy is the inverse of ambiguity:

Synonymy   Ambiguity
Paraphrase

Another view of the same relations which makes the inversion even clearer is this:

	SYNONYMY	AMBIGUITY
MEANING	**one**	**many**
FORM	**many**	**one**

These inverse relationships—ambiguity and synonymy—provide most of the evidence that grammarians use in constructing and testing syntactic hypotheses. We will later examine a larger number of rules which are intended to capture a variety of paraphrastic equivalences in English (Chapter VI). Below we list a few typical examples of complex sentences that a grammar should reveal as being related.

Consider the sentence,[4]

Computers retrieve information easily.

All the following sentences are related paraphrastically:

Information is easily retrieved by computers.
It is easy for computers to retrieve information.
Information is easy to retrieve by computers.
It is easy for information to be retrieved by computers.
Computers retrieve information with ease.
Information is retrieved by computers with ease.
For computers to retrieve information is easy.
Computers' retrieval of information is easy.
Retrieval of information by computers is easy.
Retrieving information by computers is easy.
For information to be retrieved by computers is easy.

[4] Discussed by Hutchins (1971).

To retrieve information by computers is easy.
To retrieve information is easy for computers.
Information retrieval by computers is easy.

Furthermore, the following are related to the same sentence by the addition of single constant semantic operators—and the list can be multiplied by adding such constants repeatedly to the paraphrastic versions listed above, and to each other (they of course differ in meaning by precisely that meaning contributed by the constant that is added):

NEGATION
Computers do not retrieve information easily.

INTERROGATION
Do computers retrieve information easily?

MODALITY (ability, necessity, obligation, probability . . .)
Computers can/must/should/may retrieve information easily.

QUANTIFICATION
All computers retrieve some information easily.

None of the foregoing assertions about paraphrase are intended to mean EXACT paraphrase. There probably is no such thing, ever, in any language. Distinct constructions always serve distinct semantic functions, sometimes quite subtle: matters of emphasis, or tagging what has preceded or what is to follow in the discourse. We will examine them in Chapter VI. But there is clearly a hard core of identity in the entire list. Somehow a grammar must reflect the fact that there is a situation here that is analogous to a musical theme and variations; the most fundamental semantic relationships are present in the theme, and carried over in some constant manner into all the variations.

Ambiguity of certain types poses the inverse problem. Consider the sentence,[5]

They ordered the police to stop drinking after midnight.

It can mean six distinct things:

1. They ordered the police to stop their own (the police's) drinking after midnight, on any given day.

---

[5] I owe this example to Robert B. Lees.

2. They ordered the police to stop other people from drinking after midnight on any given day.
3. They ordered the police to stop permanently all drinking of their own as of midnight.
4. They ordered the police to stop other people from any further drinking permanently from that particular midnight onward.
5. It was after midnight when they ordered the police to stop their own drinking.
6. It was after midnight when they ordered the police to stop other people's drinking.

The sentence corresponds to six different meanings. The differences do not depend on the ambiguity of particular words but only on multiple relations BETWEEN words in the sentence. A task of syntax is to show how such facts can be explained (e.g., by assigning distinct meanings to a single structure in some systematic way).

Summary of the Aims of Syntax

When we speak a sentence, or when we understand a sentence, some image of relationships between events/entities of the real world (or some imaginary or hypothetical world) may be assumed to exist in the mind. In order to characterize that mental image, let us assume the existence of a **semantic interpretation**, or **meaning**, that corresponds to it. When we put that interpretation or reading on paper, we may call it the **semantic representation** of the sentence. It is an abstract construct, always only an approximation, but it is useful in that it allows us to single out those aspects of the total meaning which are carried by the syntactic structure of sentences, as distinct from those parts that depend on the context, on the circumstances, on the particular words which a language arbitrarily correlates with actions, events, ideas, things. It is a nonlinear structure; that is, it does not exist in two-dimensional real time with units from left to right, but in some sort of multidimensional space where entities and events can be stacked in hierarchical relations (like tree-diagrams).

Given such a notion of semantic representation, the tasks of syntax can be defined as follows. Syntax specifies correspondences between semantic representations and the manifest linear strings of words in a language—i.e., which strings correspond to which representations, and what the well-formed strings are for the manifestation of a given meaning. In the course of specifying these correspondences, syntax characterizes the surface coding devices which a particular language uses, and how they work, to represent the appropriate meanings. It also specifies what devices in general are available to natural languages for this purpose.

The task of syntax looks, then, something like this:

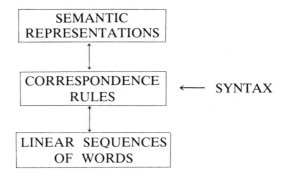

Linguists hope—and many are trying to prove—that the contents of the top box, the semantic representations, are universal. Any language has the capacity to express whatever it needs to. It is obvious that languages are most different in the contents of the bottom box, the words, word sequences, and coding devices of the language. The particular correspondence rules that we invent, our syntax, will depend heavily on our assumptions about the form of semantic representations.

Syntactic Categories

Category labels, also known as 'parts of speech', are highly traditional, going back, for the most part, to the ancient Greek and Roman grammarians. Students have never found them invigorating. There are few things a grammarian can say that seem less enlightening than that a particular word is a noun or verb or adjective. So what, if it is a noun? What are the consequences of that assertion? Most people never find out, and grammar becomes for them the dullest and least informative subject they can possibly imagine. We shall use the traditional labels, but we shall try to make them meaningful in two ways, by showing that they usually correspond to common-sense notions about the real world, and by showing that speakers really do USE categorial distinctions, though intuitively and without these particular labels, to comprehend meaning.

The effort to explain the meaning of grammatical categories like 'noun' in terms of more transparent real-world notions like 'entity' has been criticized by many grammarians. It is easy to point to words like *sincerity, abstractness, truth, beauty, goodness* and observe that while they are all nouns, there are no corresponding well-defined entities in the real world. Equally, if the category 'verb' is associated with the real-world notion 'event', it is easy to point to nouns which in fact represent events, like *death, proposal, destruction,* and conversely to point to verbs that do not appear to symbolize events, like *seem* in *He seems to be intelligent, know* in *He knows what he thinks.* In any rigid application of the equations 'noun = symbols for entities,' or 'verb = symbols for events', there is an immediate and obvious failure.

Nonetheless, an important kernel of truth remains in the equations. We can speak of *sincerity* as a property that someone *has,* we can think of it as quantifiable (*He has more sincerity than she does*), we can refer to it as a *thing* (*The thing I like best about him is his sincerity*). Indeed, thinking of nouns as symbols for entities breaks down mainly because the word *entity* itself seems to be restricted to perceivable objects. Clearly we want it to cover abstract or imaginary objects as well. It is still true, given this proviso, that the world is perceived, perhaps naively, by languages and to a large extent by speakers of languages as being divisible into two large classes: 'happenings' or 'events', on the one hand, and 'things' or 'entities' which play roles in those events, on the other. It can be argued that this is a circular perception. Things are perceived as events by speakers of a particular language because those events are generally symbolized by verbs in that language. In another language the same things might be perceived as entities because they are generally symbolized by nouns in that other language. Thus for a particular set of facts and relations in the real world—as in this drawing:

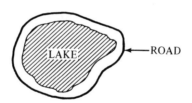

—one language might say, *There is a road running around the lake,* as English does. Another might say, *It roads around the lake,* as Navajo does. That is, it might be impossible for a particular language to predicate *run* of a road which was stationary, where another can treat a stationary road as an event.

It is certainly true in any particular instance that the correlation between grammatical nounhood and real-world entityhood, or between verbhood and eventhood, is unpredictable. But the correlation, in language after language, is so consistent that the argument seems noncircular. Events tend to be symbolized by a class of words that have unique syntactic properties. It is only this category to which temporal information (which event occurs before or after which other event?) is attached. It is only this category to which assignment of truth value in different worlds is attached (i.e., *might, can*, possible worlds, imaginary worlds, counterfactual worlds).

In the linguistic representation of an event, the central semantic notion is 'predication' of that event over some domain of entities—the 'participants' in the event. The category of words that function primarily for predication of events is the verb. Another category that functions similarly is the adjective. In languages like English, adjectives are not allowed to predicate directly in the way that verbs are; instead they are supported by the so-called **copulative** or **linking** verb *be*:

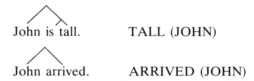

John is tall.   TALL (JOHN)

John arrived.   ARRIVED (JOHN)

The difference between adjectives and verbs, semantically, is that verbs generally predicate EVENTS whereas adjectives generally predicate STATES. There is some overlap between them, but the distinction is clear.

A possible source of confusion concerning the parts of speech is the ease with which a word may switch from one category to another. These switches are often indicated by a morphological distinction (a difference in form, such as the addition of an affix):

NOUN	ADJ	VERB
smartness	smart	smarten
redness	red	redden
anger	angry	anger
annoyance	annoyed	annoy
investigation	investigative	investigate

But not infrequently, especially in languages like English where the role of morphology is less important than it is in, say, Russian or Finnish, the switch takes place without any indication in the form of the word itself:

NOUN	VERB
The *dive* will be unsuccessful.	They will *dive* unsuccessfully.
The *debate* will last an hour.	They will *debate* for an hour.
What was the final *count*?	How many did you finally *count*?

In order to appreciate the role that is played by syntactic categories in the formation and interpretation of sentences, it is really necessary to see each category simultaneously in two ways: in relation to other categories in the surface string of words, and in relation to categories of the semantic representation of the sentence, i.e., the **semantic function** of each category.

The first of these relations—to other categories in the surface string—carries two primary kinds of information:

1. What part of the sentence is NEW information, as opposed to what part, if any, is ASSUMED TO BE FAMILIAR TO THE HEARER? That is, no conversation takes place in a vacuum. When two or more individuals interact using language, each of them makes a whole host of assumptions about the other, assumptions which are constantly tested and refined in the course of a conversation. We will see later that languages have numerous devices for indicating what the **topic** of a sentence is, for telling whether it is the same topic as in previous sentences, for informing the hearer that the topic is one that the speaker assumes the hearer is acquainted with, and so on. Languages also provide devices for directing the hearer's attention to what the speaker feels is the point, the new information, the **comment** of the sentence, and for distinguishing the topic from the comment.

2. What parts of the sentence 'go together' in a hierarchical organization? That is, in figuring out the meaning, the hearer must perceive that some relations are subordinated to others. Some are primary; others are secondary or tertiary; still others are assigned almost the status of afterthoughts. In a sentence like

   The tiresome debate finally ended.

   one can infer three predicates:

   The debate was *tiresome.*   (from *tiresome debate*)
   The debate *ended.*   (MAIN PREDICATE)
   The debate *had lasted overlong.*   (from *finally ended*)

The first and third of these predicates are clearly subordinated—or reduced to secondary status—by the use of the adjective *tiresome* and the adverb *finally*. From this example one can also see why there should be a difference between semantic categories and surface syntactic categories. The latter provide devices to represent the meaning much more compactly and economically than would be possible using only (or mainly) predicates and participants (the main categories from which a semantic representation is constructed).

The second relation between categories that must be seen clearly in order to understand their role in grammar is their semantic function. What part of the sentence is a predicate over what domain of participants? This is the cognitive aspect of meaning, the part that is interpretable as either true or false in some specified world. It is this aspect of syntactic categories that is elaborated in some detail below.

For future reference, let us give names to these two distinct functions of syntactic categories. The first we can call the **tactical** function; it enables us to perceive what goes with what, what is dominant and what is subordinate, what is assumed and what is stated. The second we can call the **cognitive** function, to represent compactly the various semantic predicates and their domains.

Syntactic Terminology

The following sections present a discussion of the principal syntactic categories, along with a rough characterization of their usual tactical and cognitive functions. These are not definitions, because only the grammar as a whole ultimately defines each category by putting it to use. That is, words which act alike in respect to all functions belong to the same category. From the point of view of the syntax, the categories are primitive concepts from which rules are constructed. The rules in turn are hypotheses about the regularities of sentence formation and interpretation. But to begin to use the terminology as it is supposed to be used, these characterizations will serve.

Verbs (V)

In their cognitive function, verbs are symbols for events (creations, changes of state, processes, actions), for states of affairs, and for speaker intention and attitude (promises, commands, hopes, expectations). In their tactical function, verbs presuppose the presence of participants (noun phrases) which function as **subjects** and **objects** of the verb (discussed under Nouns). In most—perhaps in all—languages, the following semantic concepts tend to appear with the verb in the surface form of sentences, although they are not necessarily tied directly to the verb in their meaning.

Tense. Abbreviated TE. Specifies the temporal status of the event vis-à-vis the moment of speaking. Cognitively, tense is a discourse modifier in the sense that it specifies the temporal relation that holds between the speaker and the event he is relating, not just in that one sentence but in the whole discourse of which it is a part. Tense is therefore a predicate whose domain is the entire sentence (or discourse). Taking the moment of speaking as reference point, an event may be prior to it (PAST), subsequent to it (FUTURE), or simultaneous with it (PRESENT). Past tense says, in effect, 'The event related here occurred at some time prior to the moment at which I am relating it to you.' Though all tense systems are based on the moment of speaking as the fundamental reference point, the degree to which the notions of priority, subsequence, and simultaneity may be worked out in the tense systems of particular languages varies enormously. Most languages also provide for **tenseless** assertions, i.e., those that are universally true, or generically true, or true by definition, as in *Beavers build dams.*

Aspect. Abbreviated ASP. Events take place through time; their duration may be thought of as having a beginning, a middle, and an end. One of the semantic burdens of aspectual indicators is to mark whether the event is being referred to at its initiation or termination (**perfective** aspect), or along the way between those terminals (**imperfective** aspect). Events may be marked as continuing through time (**durative** aspect) or as just beginning (**inceptive** aspect), in some languages. Although English does not mark verbs directly for these two aspects, it does provide equivalent paraphrastic constructions like *They kept working* (durative), and *They began working* (inceptive). Aspectual notions are easily confused with tense. A sentence like *John has left* specifies that the event of *leaving* is now being viewed at its completion; it is perfective (terminative) aspect in present tense. Notice that **John has left last year* is ungrammatical because *last year* assigns a time reference prior to the moment of speaking, whereas *has* assigns the aspectual reference to the moment of speaking; the two are incompatible.

Modality. Abbreviated MOD. In its cognitive function, modality relates an event to truth values in different possible worlds, worlds in which the assertion IS true (**indicative**), MIGHT be true (**possibility**), COULD be true (**ability**), MUST be true (**necessity**), and the like. The distinction between **subjunctive** and indicative, characteristic of many western languages, is of this type in some of its occurrences (e.g., *If I WERE a better grammarian, I could make this matter clearer*, where the subjunctive *were* in the first clause indicates that the statement is contrary to the facts of the real world).

Negation. Abbreviated NEG. Negation is a predication about the whole proposition that includes the verb. It predicates that the proposition is untrue. That is, a sentence like *John didn't leave* is logically equivalent to *It is not the case that John left.*

All the above—tense, aspect, modality, negation—are not infrequently attached closely to the verb, even as affixes within the verb itself; or they may be specified within the category of **auxiliary** verbs (often called 'helping verbs'), like *can, have, will* in English. It seems likely that in their semantic aspect, they are all predicates whose domain is the next lower atomic sentence in the semantic representation. Thus:

TENSE:	John arrived.	= PAST (ARRIVE (JOHN))
ASPECT:	John has arrived.	= PRES (COMPLETE (ARRIVE (JOHN)))
MODALITY:	John may arrive.	= POSSIBLE (ARRIVE (JOHN))
NEGATION:	John didn't arrive.	= NOT (PAST (ARRIVE (JOHN)))

This appears in tree form (simplified considerably) on p. 41.

Not uncommonly, the verb also contains some marker that determines the **focus** of the predication—that is, it determines which of the several entity words associated with it is to be taken as information shared by the speaker and hearer, and which is to be taken as new information, placed in the foreground of attention. For example, the verbs *buy* and *sell* are the inverse of each other in this respect:

John bought the watch from Bill.
  (*Bill* is foregrounded, new information.)
Bill sold the watch to John.
  (*John* is foregrounded, new information.)

While English does not characteristically mark focus in the verb and so does not serve well for exemplification, perhaps the most striking property of languages of the Malayo-Polynesian family like Tagalog (the national language of the Philippines) is the uniform manner in which focus is marked in virtually every verb. We will examine the notions of 'focus' and 'topic' further in Chapter VI.

Verb Phrase. Abbreviated VP. Verb phrases are clusters of words in surface strings of which the nuclei are verbs. The surface satellites around the verb include not only tense, aspect, modality, and negation (all of which are semantically higher predicates), but also noun phrases that

SURFACE

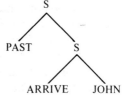

SEMANTIC REPRESENTATION

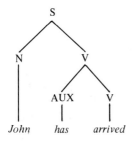

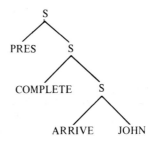

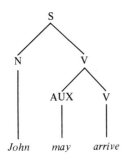

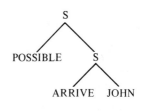

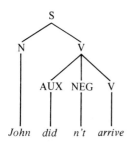

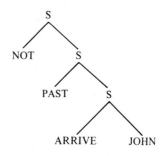

refer to the participants in the event specified by the verb (agents, goals, objects, patients, instruments, and the like).

In some kinds of syntactic analysis, the verb plus its complements is considered to be the **predicate** of a sentence—i.e., everything except the subject. This usage merely substitutes the term 'predicate' for the category label VP, since the predication, in a semantic sense, is specified by the 'verb' over a domain that includes BOTH the grammatical subject and the grammatical objects. That is, the unit VP has no independent semantic interpretation, since it is not interpreted as a unit apart from the subject.

Adverbs (ADV)

The name suggests that adverbs (including most prepositional phrases) function as modifiers of verbs (*ad* = 'to, toward'), which is indeed a principal tactical function of many types of adverbs—they are subordinated directly to the verb:

Locative adverbs (LOC) specify the place where an event occurs or where a state is said to exist:

> John died *in bed.*
> John works *at home.*

Temporal adverbs are of two primary types: 'durative' and 'point time'. **Durative** adverbs (DUR) specify the duration of an event:

> John worked *for two hours.*
> Rip Van Winkle slept *for twenty years.*

Or, depending on the nature of the event, a durative adverb may impose an iterative interpretation on the event (i.e., the event happened over and over again during the specified time span):

> John wrote letters *all night long.*
> He practiced the sonata *for a year.*

Point time adverbs (TM) specify the time at which an event began or, if taken as a whole, occurred:

> John ate *at six o'clock.*
> John fell down *yesterday.*

Frequency adverbs (FREQ) can perhaps be considered a type of **quantifier**—they quantify events in the way that numerals quantify entities:

> John proposed to Mary *three times.*
> = Mary received *three proposals* of marriage from John.
> John proposed to Mary *every day.*
> John proposed to Mary *on alternate Fridays.*

Directional adverbs (DIR) are so closely attached to their verbs that they might better be considered as complements (like direct objects), and this closeness is sometimes substantiated by the fact that there is a corresponding verb that incorporates the directionality within its own semantics:

> He pulled the piston *from the sleeve.*
> = He *extracted* the piston from the sleeve.
> He rammed the bullet *into the cylinder.*
> = He *inserted* the bullet into the cylinder.

But although the adverbs listed above serve as verb modifiers in their tactical function and could reasonably be argued to be much the same in their cognitive function, many other phrases that are traditionally called adverbs bear only a tactical relationship to the verb. Their cognitive relationship is to a larger domain: the verb AND its subject. Consider the example discussed earlier, *John plays beautifully. Beautifully* would usually be called a **manner** adverb (MAN), but we saw that the adverb was semantically the main predicate (i.e., roughly, JOHN'S PLAYING IS BEAUTIFUL). There are other types of adverbs where this analysis— namely, that adverbs function cognitively as predicates over some domain larger than the verb—is appealing:

> She is *obviously* intelligent.
> = *It is obvious* that she is intelligent.
> He is *apparently* stupid.
> = *It appears* that he is stupid.
> He is *probably* right.
> = *It is probable* that he is right.
> *Admittedly*, I might be wrong.
> = *I admit* that I might be wrong.

In all such cases, what appears to be the main sentence in the surface forms (*She is intelligent, He is stupid, He is right, I might be wrong*) is semantically interpreted as a complement of the adverb, which is itself the main predicate:

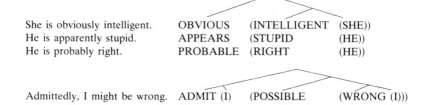

She is obviously intelligent.	OBVIOUS	(INTELLIGENT	(SHE))
He is apparently stupid.	APPEARS	(STUPID	(HE))
He is probably right.	PROBABLE	(RIGHT	(HE))

| Admittedly, I might be wrong. | ADMIT (I) | (POSSIBLE | (WRONG (I))) |

These adverbs—*obviously, apparently, probably, admittedly*—are often called **sentential** adverbs because they seem to modify whole sentences. They are simply predicates whose congnitive domain is a proposition—that is, they make a predication about the whole proposition (THAT SHE IS INTELLIGENT IS A PROPOSITION WHICH IS OBVIOUSLY TRUE = *It is obvious that she is intelligent*). They differ from manner adverbs in that manner adverbs are predicates over events (HIS PLAYING IS BEAUTIFUL). In both types the semantic structure, the basis for the semantic interpretation is, at least roughly, the same:

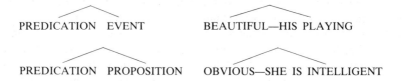

PREDICATION EVENT   BEAUTIFUL—HIS PLAYING

PREDICATION PROPOSITION   OBVIOUS—SHE IS INTELLIGENT

The fact that both manner adverbs and sentential adverbs are transparently predicates suggests that other adverbs may also be profitably analyzed as predicates in their cognitive functions. Consider again the sentences *John died in bed* and *John works at home.* They are not necessarily locative in their interpretation at all:

> John died in bed.
> = John died while he was in bed.
>   John died when he was in bed.
>   It was in bed that John died.

> John works at home.
> = John works while he is at home.
>   John works when he is at home.
>   It is at home (not at the office) that John does his work.

In each case, the first two interpretations are temporal, not locative. Only the third interpretation is unambiguously locative. But this unambiguous locative interpretation requires the same kind of predicate-plus-complement structure that is required for sentential adverbs:

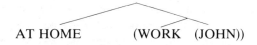

AT HOME   (WORK   (JOHN))

Durative adverbs show similar properties; i.e., they are interpreted as predicates over events:

John slept *for two hours.*

= John's sleeping $\left\{\begin{array}{l} \textit{went on} \\ \textit{lasted} \\ \textit{endured} \end{array}\right\}$ *for two hours.*

That is, durative adverbs imply a predicate like *last, endure, go on, persist* for a specified period of time, with reference to some event. Point time adverbs are similar except that they imply a predicate like *begin, happen,* or *occur:*

John ate *at six o'clock.*
= John's eating *began at six o'clock.*
John fell down *yesterday.*
= John's falling down *happened yesterday.*

Still other categories of adverbs imply predications over events. **Instrumental** adverbs, for example, suggest a predicate like *make use of, use:*

John opened the safe *with a blowtorch.*
= John *used a blowtorch* to open the safe.

There is a problem of intentionality in this interpretation; while it is clear that if John used a blowtorch to open a safe, he meant to do so, it is not so clear that intentionality is implied by examples like this:

John nicked his face *with a razor.*
= ?? John *used a razor* to nick his face.

But in such examples, where the sense is more like *John's face got nicked with a razor,* or even *A razor nicked John's face,* it is likely that *John* is not to be understood as an agent making use of an instrument at all. That is, the absence of intention on the part of the agent also eliminates the instrumental interpretation of the adverb; it can be interpreted instead as an adverb of **means**.

It should by now be apparent that the category 'adverb' is a very loose one in grammatical usage. We have scratched the surface of adverbial complexity in order to show that some adverbs, in their cognitive functions, are special kinds of predicates over events, over actions, or over propositions; other adverbs do not appear to be predicates at all, but rather to be types of complements (directional adverbs); still others appear to be closely related to comparative constructions (the **intensifiers**, below); still others provide background or motivation for the action set forth in the main predication (**purpose**, **causal**, **transitional** adverbs, below). Following is a partial classification of types of adverbs based on their cognitive functions.

PREDICATIONS OVER EVENTS OR ACTIONS

LOCATIVE

> John works *at home.*
> = *It is at home* that John works.

DURATIVE

> Rip Van Winkle slept *for twenty years.*
> = Rip Van Winkle's sleeping *lasted for twenty years.*

POINT TIME

> John fell down *yesterday.*
> = John's falling down *happened yesterday.*

MANNER

> John plays *beautifully.*
> = John's playing *is beautiful.*

MEANS

> He solved the problem *with the help of his friends.*
> = He *made use of the help of his friends* in solving the problem.

INSTRUMENTAL

> He opened the safe *with a blowtorch.*
> = He *used a blowtorch* to open the safe.

ACCOMPANIMENT

> He went to the movies *with Mary.*
> = He *accompanied Mary* to the movies.
> He and Mary *accompanied each other* in going to the movies.

PREDICATIONS OVER PROPOSITIONS

FACTIVE[1]

Admittedly, he is a fool.
= *I admit it is a fact* that he is a fool.

Obviously she is intelligent.
= *It is a fact obvious to anyone* that she is intelligent.

MODALITY

He will *possibly* arrive tomorrow.
= *There is a possible world,* in this case the future one known as 'tomorrow', in which his arrival will occur.

He would *normally* have played the sonata faster.
= *In a world that can be described as 'normal',* which is not the current state of affairs, his playing of the sonata would have required less time than it in fact did.

QUANTIFIERS AND COMPARATIVES[2]

FREQUENCY

John *often* works late.
= Relative to some norm, the action of working late *occurs with a frequency* in John's behavior *that noticeably exceeds the norm.*

INTENSIFIER

John is *quite* tired.
= Relative to some norm of tiredness, John's condition *exceeds it substantially.*

COMPARATIVE

Jane is *more beautiful* than Mary.
= *The extent of* Jane's beauty *exceeds the extent of* Mary's beauty.

PREDICATIONS OF MOTIVATIONS, CONDITIONS, TRANSITIONS

PURPOSE

John moonlights *to make ends meet.*
= *John's purpose* in holding two jobs *is to make ends meet.*

---

[1] The term 'factive' refers to a certain presupposition of the speaker who uses one of these predicates, namely that the proposition of the predicate is a fact. Thus, *I (don't) regret that John is leaving* presupposes that John is leaving, whether I regret it or not.

[2] Both are predications over quantities, definite and indefinite.

CAUSE

> John took up the cello *because he was bored with golf.*
> = *The cause of John's action* of taking up the cello *was his boredom with golf.*

CONDITIONAL

> *If five students show up,* the class will be held.
> = *The condition* on holding the class *is that five students must show up.*

> *If we had world enough and time,* we would read more metaphysical poetry.
> = *The condition* on our reading more metaphysical poetry *is the (counterfactual) condition that we would have to be less busy than we are.*

TRANSITIONAL

> *Nevertheless,* I'll read whatever I want to.
> = *In spite of what has just been asserted,* I'll read whatever I want to.

> *On the other hand,* that might be a form of suicide.
> = *An alternative interpretation of the previous assertion* is that it might be suicidal.

Nouns (N)

In their cognitive function, nouns are symbols for entities, abstract or concrete, countable or uncountable (masses), animate or inanimate, human or nonhuman. These properties are arranged in a natural hierarchy:

If HUMAN   (e.g., *man* vs. *animal*)

   then⎱ANIMATE   (e.g., *animal* vs. *rock*)
    if ⎰

      then⎱COUNTABLE   (e.g., *rocks* vs. *trash*)
      if ⎰

         then CONCRETE   (e.g., *trash* vs. *sincerity*)

These are INHERENT features of nouns which play a role in the determination of compatibility with verbs. For example, inanimate nouns are semantically strange with verbs that presuppose animate participants:

? The rocks laughed.
? The rubbish frolicked.

But why select these particular semantic features of nouns for grammatical discussion? The range of semantic features that are relevant in the same way is very wide. For example,

DURATIVE TIME (vs. POINT TIME)

An hour elapsed.
? One o'clock elapsed.
?? The tree elapsed.

LIQUIDITY (vs. SOLIDITY)

They immersed him in water.
?? They immersed him in stone.
He drank the milk.
?? He drank the steak.

FLEXIBILITY (vs. INFLEXIBILITY of various types)

He wrinkled the paper.
?? He wrinkled the theory.
?? He wrinkled the granite.

By metaphorical extension, we can make sense of many such violations, e.g., *He didn't demolish the theory completely, but he wrinkled it a bit,* and indeed literary praise is often bestowed on precisely those instances where a surprising juxtaposition of this sort is achieved:

... how sweetly flows
That liquefaction of her clothes   (Robert Herrick)

Now folds the lily all her sweetness up   (Alfred Tennyson)

The rosemary nods upon the grave   (Edgar Allan Poe)

Thou still unravish'd bride of quietness   (John Keats)

Full many a flower is born to blush unseen   (Thomas Gray)

Clothes are not liquid, lilies cannot fold anything, rosemaries do not nod, quietness has no bride, flowers do not blush—all of which only means that the skillful user of language knows how to transfer (or extend) meanings from their natural or literal domain into metaphorical domains. And when such transfers are especially striking or felicitous, they are highly valued.

Why, then, are the semantic features 'human', 'animate', 'count-able', and 'concrete' so commonly mentioned in grammars when others are not? The answer appears to be that these particular inherent features have consequences of a rather pervasive sort in the syntax of many languages. For example, in English, the feature 'human' is associated with a special form of the relative pronoun:

The boy $\left\{ \begin{matrix} \text{whom} \\ \text{*which} \end{matrix} \right\}$ we encountered . . .

The problem $\left\{ \begin{matrix} \text{which} \\ \text{*whom} \end{matrix} \right\}$ we encountered . . .

$\left. \begin{matrix} \text{The boy} \\ \text{The problem} \end{matrix} \right\}$ that we encountered . . .

The feature 'animate' is required of nouns for entities that can serve as experiencers of emotions and the like (*anger, annoyance, distemper*), and many languages mark such relationships in a way grammatically distinct from 'performing' kinds of predications. Old English, for example, could not say *I like to make money*, but only the equivalent of *It pleases me to make money*—and such verbs could occur only with animate nouns. The feature 'count' is tied up in complex ways with the rules for the formation of plurals, so that uncountable nouns can be made plural only in round-about ways:

COUNTABLE		UNCOUNTABLE	
SINGULAR	PLURAL	SINGULAR	QUANTIFIED PHRASE
ocean	oceans	water	glasses of water
lake	lakes		(*waters* occurs only in a special meaning— 'waters of Lake Michigan')
glacier	glaciers	ice	blocks of ice (*ices* means 'types of ice')
suitcase	suitcases	luggage	pieces of luggage

The feature 'concrete' is involved in the rules which govern classes of verbal complements:

$$\text{He persuaded her} \begin{cases} \text{to study.} \\ \text{of the truth.} \end{cases}$$

$$\text{*He persuaded her of} \begin{cases} \text{Bill.} \\ \text{the boy.} \\ \text{the table.} \end{cases}$$

Let us assume, then, that the characterization of the meaning of every noun must include certain features that are more general—more common or widespread in the language—than others, and that these features sometimes are used by the syntactic rules of languages.

It is useful to distinguish between **nouns** and **nominals**, where 'nominal' refers to nounlike words or phrases that are not actually headed by a noun:

The poor are always with us.

where *poor* is a nominalized adjective. Nominalization is a syntactic process of great generality whereby words or phrases or clauses are made to function as though the entire group were a single noun. Thus each of the phrases or clauses in italics below is an instance of nominalization:

He eats *whatever he wants to.*
i.e., He eats something.
He took the high road, I took *the low.*
i.e., the low road
He said (*that*) *he was leaving.*
i.e., He said something.
He told me *when he was leaving.*
i.e., He told me a time or a date.
He asked me *where I was going.*
i.e., He asked me the name of my destination

In some theories, this process is known as **rank-shifting**; categories like 'noun', 'verb', 'adjective' are assigned a primary rank. Longer phrases or clauses which would in their primary function be full predications can be thought of as having been demoted to the secondary functional status of single words belonging to these various syntactic categories.

Nominalization is more common, in languages of the world, than the analogous process of **verbalization** (forming verbs from nonverb categories), though within the lexicon there typically are productive processes by which verbs may be formed from nouns; in English, we have *edit* from *editor*, *to truck* from the noun *truck*, *instantiate* from *instance*, and the like. On a scale from actions, events, or processes at the one extreme to concrete, observable, touchable objects at the other, 'verbs' typically symbolize the former and 'nouns' the latter. The two basic building blocks of all sentences in all languages are verbs and nouns.

Noun Functions

Since there are never enough verbs to symbolize all possible events, full predications are built up through the use of **complements**, composed of noun phrases, attached to verbs to form verb phrases. The notion 'complement' can be clarified if we consider the difference between **intransitive** predications and **transitive** ones. An intransitive predication is one which is made about only one participant, the subject:

$$
\text{The queen} \begin{cases} \text{slept.} \\ \text{ran.} \\ \text{arrived.} \\ \text{died.} \\ \text{left.} \end{cases}
$$

Now, if the predication is one which can only be made about two participants, it is a transitive predication, and the second participant is a type of verb complement called a **direct object**:

$$
\text{The queen} \begin{cases} \text{loves} \\ \text{killed} \\ \text{answered} \\ \text{divorced} \\ \text{left} \end{cases} \text{the king.}
$$

Notice that *left* appears in both lists; this shows that the notion 'transitive' is not a property of a word *qua* word but rather of a semantic concept REPRESENTED by a word. The notion *leave* in *The queen left the king* is a transitive one, whereas *leave* in the sense of *depart* is intransitive. Conversely, the following sentences all contain transitive predications even though no direct object is formally present:

$$\text{The student} \begin{cases} \text{drinks.} \\ \text{smokes.} \\ \text{reads.} \\ \text{tries.} \end{cases}$$

The point, then, is that the addition (or implication) of an object (one type of complement) to a transitive verb makes that whole transitive verb phrase complete and therefore equivalent to an intransitive verb phrase, in the sense that they are equally fulfilled with respect to their logical potential:

ONE-PLACE PREDICATE (e.g., *arrive*)

= INTRANSITIVE
= SUBJECT + VERB
=   NP   + VP

TWO-PLACE PREDICATE (e.g., *love*)

= TRANSITIVE (single-object)
= SUBJECT + VERB + OBJECT
=   NP   + $\underbrace{\text{V} + \text{NP}}$
=   NP   +   VP

Similarly other multiple-place predicates:

THREE-PLACE PREDICATE (e.g., *give*)

= TRANSITIVE (double-object)
= SUBJECT + VERB + OBJECT$_1$ + OBJECT$_2$
=   NP   + $\underbrace{\text{V} + \text{NP} + \text{NP}}$
=   NP   +   VP

There are a few predicates that do not have logical subjects at all, even though languages like English may supply an empty subject for them:

It's raining/snowing/storming/hailing . . .

The *it* of such expressions has no referent unless one wants to argue that the sentence is really

The weather is raining/snowing/storming/hailing . . .

Likewise the *there* of expressions like

There's a party at ten o'clock tonight.

is not to be easily identified as a subject, nor is the *es* of German expressions like

Es gibt   ein Problem.
it gives a   problem
There is a problem.

Many languages have single-unit expressions for notions like *there is...* For example,

Hay   *unos   libros   aqui.*   (Spanish)
there $\begin{Bmatrix} \text{is} \\ \text{are} \end{Bmatrix}$ some   books   here

May   *libro   sa   mesa.*   (Tagalog)
there $\begin{Bmatrix} \text{is} \\ \text{are} \end{Bmatrix}$ book   on   table

For such expressions, it is probably simplest to set up a logical notion of 'zero-place' predicates—i.e., predications without any participants: just events, or states of affairs.

Reference in Nouns

One crucial link must now be made between predications and their interpretations in the real world. Verbs symbolize actions, states, and relations between participants; participants in turn are identified by nouns. But nouns like *boy, table, event, sincerity, stone* DO NOT REFER TO THE WORLD OUTSIDE in and of themselves. Who does *boy* refer to? What does *table* refer to? In order to make a link between most predications and some actual event, there must be some **referring** expression inside the predication. Referring expressions are of several types:

1. Those with inherent reference:

   proper nouns (*John, John Harrington Smith, The Rocky Mountains,* ...)

2. Those with stipulated reference:

   that boy whom you met last night

3. Those that refer to members of a class:

   Boys are amusing. = 'All individuals belonging to the class of young homo sapiens males are amusing.'

4. Those that refer back (**anaphoric** reference) to some previous mention, or are understood from common knowledge:

   John left early. *He* was tired.

5. Those that designate the speaker (*I*) and hearer (*you*).

Actually, proper names are instances of stipulated reference, stipulated by a list (in your memory, in a phone directory, in the United States Census—anywhere that says, in effect, 'the name XXX is taken to refer uniquely to such and such an individual').

It is by means of the independently referring character of proper names, and of nouns that are stipulated to refer to particular individuals or classes of individuals, that language links itself to the reality of the outside world. All languages are therefore very rich in devices to stipulate the reference of nouns, and to refer back to individuals whose identity has already been established. These devices are found in the **noun phrase**.

Noun Phrases (NP)

Noun phrases are clusters of words in surface strings of which the nuclei are nouns. In their cognitive functions, noun phrases can be independently referring expressions. In their tactical functions, they are subjects and objects of predicators. The satellites around the noun nucleus are various categories of **determiners** (DET) which serve to stipulate the reference of the noun. Determiners bear much the same relation to nouns that auxiliaries bear to verbs. Certain semantic information normally clusters with verbs—tense, frequency, negative/positive polarity, modality, aspect—because such information has to do most directly with the nature of actions/events/processes (when they occurred, how often, whether they occurred or not, whether they really occurred at all or only in some other possible world might have occurred, etc.). Similarly, certain other semantic information normally clusters with nouns, usually in subcategories of determiners (**articles**, **quantifiers**, and **deictics**, discussed below), but also by the use of other syntactic devices such as word order. Let us consider first the kinds of semantic and referential information that serve to stipulate noun reference and thereby link predications to the world outside of language.

Definiteness. The categories **definite article** (*the*) and **indefinite article** (*a, some, . . .*) are among the less transparent ones found in grammars. The notion 'definite' has to do with a number of possible semantic dimensions. Perhaps the most common one is **previous mention**. Previous mention has all sorts of syntactic consequences, among which the use of definite articles (or some other definitizing device) is just one. The most far-reaching consequence of previous mention is the complete replacement of noun phrases by short substitute (anaphoric) words called **pronouns**.

All languages provide some device for stipulating that a certain NP is being introduced into the discourse for the first time, and if the language makes a distinction between 'definite' and 'indefinite', the introducing expression applies always to the indefinite form of the NP:

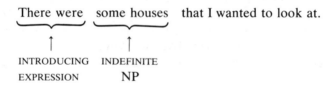

This is very much like the logical notation ∃, as in

$\exists x P(x)$
'There exists some *x*, such that the proposition *P* is true of that *x*.'

In general, the first mention of a particular object or idea requires the indefinite article in languages which make the distinction by the use of articles:

> John bought *a house.*
> (His purchase has not been previously mentioned; it is here introduced into the discourse for the first time.)
> Was *the house* very expensive?
> (The indefinite article can no longer be used, because the conversation is continuing on the basis of previous mention of the house.)

Now suppose the conversation continues in the following vein:

> Are they giving up *the apartment*?

But the apartment has not been previously mentioned; since the definite article is used, we must assume that it is an apartment which both speakers are familiar with. That is, another basis for definiteness, besides previous mention, is **common knowledge** (common, at least, to the participants in the discourse). At the very least, when a speaker uses a definite form, it is clear that he **presupposes** that his hearer is familiar with it, and if his presupposition turns out to be incorrect, we can get exchanges like the following:

A. I saw *the television show.* It was great.
B. *What* television show? I don't remember suggesting that you watch a particular one.
A. Oh, wasn't it you who told me to be sure to watch it? Must have been Joe.

Common knowledge may also be extended to account for the definite article with nouns like *sun, moon, president.* We would normally not talk about *a sun* or *a moon* except in a context, as in an astronomy class, where more than one referent was possible. Unless the context makes some other choice more likely, *the president* will refer to the president of the United States. The two concepts, 'previous mention' and 'common knowledge', can be subsumed under a single term, **common focus**, which has the further virtue of including the third feature which is characteristic of definiteness, namely that it is often the topic on which the predication is focused. That is, it characteristically presents background, or given, or presupposed, or already known, information:

When is *the party?*
(It is already known that there is to be a party—that is given or presupposed information; the query is about the time or date.)
Let's have *a party.*
(No party has been planned, and *have a party* is the new information, the main predication.)

Let's consider *the other solution.*
(Exactly two have been proposed.)
Let's consider *another solution.*
(It has not been proposed yet; presumably it is about to be, and this sentence introduces it.)

Languages that do not have definite/indefinite articles often use deictics— 'pointing' words like *this, that, these, those*—for definiteness whenever word order will not serve. In the history of many languages, including

English, definite articles are derived from deictics. Indefinite articles are usually derived from the number *one* (it is not hard to see that *a/an* are related to it, and in Spanish, the forms of the number and of the indefinite article are identical—*un, uno, unos*). We will return in Chapter III to the question of how word order is used by many languages to mark the definite/indefinite contrast.

Quantification. Both entities and events can be counted; the function of frequency adverbs, we have noted, is to provide for the counting of events. Quantifiers serve that function with nouns. It is not uncommon to find, as in English, three distinct kinds of quantification:

1. Where the noun represents a countable object (*boy, girl, house, dish, idea*), we find numbers (*one, two, three, . . .*), the universal quantifiers (e.g., *all, every*), indefinite quantifiers (*several, some, certain, [a] few, various, many*), and enumerators (*each, both*):

   two boys, many girls, various suggestions, several ideas, . . .
   but not
   *two garbages, *many luggages, *various informations, *several milks

2. With nouns that represent uncountable substances or objects and with many abstract nouns, we find partitive quantifiers (e.g., *much, a lot of, some*) and the universal quantifier (*all*), but no numbers, indefinite quantifiers, or enumerators:

   a lot of garbage, much luggage, considerable information, several glasses of milk

3. A third kind of quantifier includes the ordinal numbers and expressions of evaluation: *first, last, principal, main, best, ...* Many adjectivelike words appear in this set, but they do not have the predicative quality of true adjectives:

   The late president . . .
   *The president is late.

   The principal reason . . .
   *The reason is principal.

   The other complaint . . .
   *The complaint is other.

We have now considered three subcategories of the determiner—namely, articles (definite and indefinite), deictics, and quantifiers—that serve to stipulate the reference of nouns. These devices do not often appear along with proper names, because the reference of any name is—in principle, though of course not actually in practice—a single, unique individual. Thus, in English both *the* and *a* can be used if there is more than one individual who might be referred to by a certain proper name, but not otherwise:

> *The Mary went home early.
> The Mary that I played bridge with last night went home early; the Mary that I had dinner with was impossible to get rid of.

> *A Mary would know the answer.
> A Mary would know what it's like to be the namesake of the mother of Jesus; but how could an Elizabeth understand?

When the reference of a noun cannot be clarified satisfactorily by any determiner, then languages use a device known as the **relative clause**, which is a sentence embedded into a noun phrase, and marked in some way as subordinate to the particular noun for which clarity of reference is sought. It is commonly assumed in grammars that there are two kinds of relative clauses, called by various names:

> TYPE 1: **Restrictive Clauses**
> The book *that I read last night* was dull.

> TYPE 2: **Appositive (Nonrestrictive, Attributive) Clauses**
> The book, *which I read last night,* was dull.

Only type 1 clauses serve to stipulate the reference of nouns. Type 2 clauses simply provide additional information—they can be omitted without losing track of the reference of any NP. The relevant ones, then, the so-called **restrictive relative clauses**, could be more appropriately designated 'stipulatory clauses' or 'referential clauses' or the like. Note that the relative clause can be considerably 'reduced' (i.e., some material can be deleted from it) without destroying its stipulative function:

> The girl *who is pretty* . . .
> = The *pretty* girl . . .

> The book *that is on the table* . . .
> = The book *on the table* . . .

Predication vs. Participation

We have seen how some NP's achieve independently referring status; that is the purpose served by the machinery of determiners and relative clauses. This might be thought of as the 'outward-looking' aspect of NP's—how they relate to the real world. But they also have an 'inward-looking' aspect, namely how they relate to the predicator. There are three ways in which information about this relation is carried by natural languages: (1) word order, (2) affixes, and (3) specialized function words, called **adpositions** (**prepositions** and **postpositions**). We will examine word-order devices more closely in Chapter III. For the moment we need note only the obvious facts that in English, for example, the subject-NP normally precedes a transitive predicator whereas the object-NP normally follows it, and that in most such sentences the fixed order is the only way one can tell which is which. This piece of information is also present, in the same way, in logical formulas. Whether we write $P(x, y)$, as in *studies* (*the class, astronomy*), or $(x)P(y)$, as in (*the class*) *studies* (*astronomy*), the predicate P applies to the first participant as subject and the second as object, in all transitive relations (*hit, cut, create, change, make*, etc.).

Affixes and adpositions are two syntactic manifestations of one single semantic phenomenon. The difference between them is superficial and formal: affixes are part of the noun and cannot be separated from it as independently pronounceable words (like the plural affix—*boy/boys, house/houses*), whereas adpositions are independent words (*to, for, by, from*, etc.). In languages like Latin, there was a regular set of affixes to mark what are known as 'case' relationships between NP and verb:

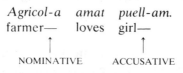

Agricol-a   amat   puell-am.
farmer—   loves   girl—
↑   ↑
NOMINATIVE   ACCUSATIVE

The farmer loves the girl.

'Nominative' is the name of a case which says, of the noun to which it is attached, 'This noun is functioning as SUBJECT of the main predication.' 'Accusative' says 'This noun is functioning as DIRECT OBJECT of the main predication.' Given these case-markers, the nouns could appear in any order, without ambiguity:

Agricola puellam amat.
Amat puellam agricola.
Puellam amat agricola.
Puellam agricola amat.

In fact, the case-marking system of Classical Latin was a rather inefficient one which led to various changes in the subsequent history of the Romance languages, but it serves to illustrate the way a case-marking system CAN work. Case-marking does not have to take the form of suffixes. The cases may be prefixed, infixed, suffixed, or, as suggested above, they may take the form of separate function words, 'prepositions' or 'postpositions', depending on whether they precede the NP, as in English, or follow it, as in Japanese.

The question is: What are these case-marking devices, whether affixes or adpositions, DOING for the NP? The answer that seems most plausible is, They are **lower predicates**—i.e., predicates that are subordinate to the main predicate expressed by the verb—and what they do is STIPULATE EXPLICITLY WHAT THE ROLE OF THE NP PARTICIPANT IS IN THE HIGHER PREDICATE. Another way (perhaps equivalent) of characterizing the function of case-marking devices is to say that they are predicates over a complex domain consisting of (1) the NP to which they are attached, and (2) the main predicate:

K (NP, Pred)

Thus if K (case) is, say, 'dative', this expression would be defined to mean that 'the NP functions as receiver of the action expressed by Pred', and similarly for each possible case relation $K_1, K_2, K_3, \ldots K_n$. Consider a sentence with several case-marked NP's:

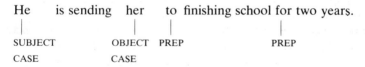

This can be paraphrased—i.e., its semantic organization can be more specifically suggested—in this way:

The act of sending is *by him.* (*he* in 'subject case')
The act of sending applies *to her.* (*her* in 'object case')
The action is *directed to* the finishing school. (*to* marking the goal)
Her stay *will last* two years. (*for* marking duration)

Another way of paraphrasing the relations might be this:

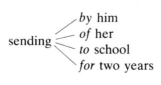

The need for case-marking affixes and adpositions in noun phrases arises from the fact that an event/action can apply to different entities, be related to different entities, in a variety of ways, and the essence of an assertion or proposition is the specification of these relationships. The variety and functions of case-marking will be dealt with in more detail in Chapter III. For now, it is sufficient to understand that they are economical predicates which function to relate participants (NP's) to main predicators in several ways.

Summary of Syntactic Terminology

We have now seen in rough form the main syntactic categories and some of their functions, both tactical and cognitive. The number of distinct categories is actually quite small:

Noun	Verb
Article/Deictic	Adjective
Quantifier	Adverb
Pre ⎫ position	
Post ⎭	Auxiliary

Traditional lists of the 'parts of speech' also include **interjections** like *oh, ah, ouch,* and various **particles** like *yes.*

The number of distinct semantic functions is quite large, including not only subject, direct object, indirect object, complement, but also all the adverbial types, the determiner functions within NP's, the tense/modality/aspect functions within VP's, the relational functions of case-markers and adpositions, and others that will come up in subsequent discussion.

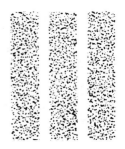

Surface Syntactic Information

From the most superficial point of view, a sentence is a string of words proceeding from now to then through time, or from left to right on the page (in various orthographies from right to left, top to bottom, bottom to top, or some combination of these—in all instances, the conventional placement of words on the page is merely an index of progression through time). Two strings made up of the same basic set of words may differ in only a small number of ways:

1. **Serial Order.** The words may occur in different serial orders:

I sprayed *the wall green.*
I sprayed *the green wall.*

Help *me find* a job.
Help *find me* a job.

Man bites dog.
Dog bites man.

That is impossible *even* for John.
Even that is impossible for John.

John *has* a lot of work *to do.*
John *has to do* a lot of work.

2. **Morphology.** The words may occur in the same order but in different forms, i.e., with different affixes (or, equivalently, with different adpositions):

Agricola   puellam   amat.   (Latin)
farmer-NOM   girl-ACCUS   loves
The farmer loves the girl.

Agricolam   puella   amat.
farmer-ACCUS   girl-NOM   loves
The girl loves the farmer.

Zaeni   maerdi   busid.   (Persian)
woman   man   kissed
A woman kissed a man.

Zaeni-ra   maerdi   busid.
woman-GOAL   man   kissed
A man kissed a woman.

B-um-abasa   ng-diyaryo   ang-titser.   (Tagalog)
is reading   NONFOCUS-newspaper   FOCUS-teacher
um = FOCUS ON ACTOR
The teacher is reading a newspaper.

B-in-abasa   ang-diyaryo   ng-titser.
is reading   FOCUS-newspaper   NONFOCUS-teacher
in = FOCUS ON GOAL
The teacher is reading the newspaper.
The newspaper is being read by the teacher.

John saw Mary leave.
John saw Mary leav**ing**.

John hates work.
John hates **to** work.

The door was open.
The door was open**ed**.

1. + 2. **Serial Order plus Morphology.** The first two may be combined: the words may occur in different orders along with different function markers:

> *Agricola   puellam   amat.*
> farmer-NOM   girl-ACCUS   loves
> The farmer loves the girl.

> *Puella   agricolam   amat.*
> girl-NOM   farmer-ACCUS loves
> The girl loves the farmer.

3. **Intonation and Phrasing.** Although the same word order is maintained, words may be grouped into different clusters by features of intonation (pitch of voice, indicated in the following examples by italics for higher pitch) and tempo (spacing, indicated by a dash):

> They decorated the *girl*—with the *flowers.*
> = They used the flowers as decoration for the girl.
> They *decorated*—the girl with the *flowers.*
> = They identified her by virtue of the fact that she had some flowers, and they decorated her with something else.

> The guests departed *regretfully.*
> = The guests were regretful about departing.
> The guests *departed*, regretfully.
> = I regret that the guests departed.

> The *new*—World *Football* league
> The new *world*—*football* league

> The car my father bought at *last*—needed *repairs.*
> The car my father *bought*—at last needed *repairs.*

4. **Syntactic Categories.** The words may belong to different syntactic categories. This sometimes, though rarely, occurs as the ONLY difference:

> V   N   ADV
> Ship sails today.

> N   V   ADV
> Ship sails today.

Category membership usually requires either word-order change (1 above), or overt marking (2), or both; and it may be accompanied by intonational differences (3). Some examples:

N   V   N
John loves beauty.

N   V   ADV
John loves beautifully. (2 and 4)

N   V   N
Violence   strikes work
(Newspaper headline: 'Violence erupts and stops work from proceeding.')

ADJ   N   V
Violent strikes work. (2, 3, and 4)
(Newspaper headline: 'Strikes that are violent are successful.'

All information about the meaning of sentences must somehow be derived from these four sources, plus two others that are not the direct concern of syntax: choice of words, and nonlinguistic context. Choice of words is to some extent a concern of syntax because of dependency relations (Chapter I), but in the sense that a word is chosen because its meaning corresponds to some mental image which the speaker wants to communicate, the choice of words is independent of syntax. Nonlinguistic context is also independent of syntax even though it may affect both word choice and syntactic arrangement by virtue of the presuppositions and external truth conditions that it imposes. The way in which we talk about some object that both speaker and hearer can see right there in front of them is very different from the way we talk about objects not present in the immediate environment. We now consider these four sources in more detail to see what kinds of information they contribute to the unraveling of semantic interpretations from linear strings of words.

Serial Order of Words

The most obvious, and linguistically most trivial, contribution of serial order is to be seen in examples where the event which is stated first also happened first—that is, the temporal order of words corresponds directly to the temporal order of events:

John went home and had dinner.
John had dinner and went home.

Jane got married and became pregnant.
Jane became pregnant and got married.

Bill invested in stocks and became a millionaire.
Bill became a millionaire and invested in stocks.

Although it is clear that this correspondence between serial order and meaning does exist, linguists would not count it as a significant syntactic property of serial order. It is no more than a useful, and universal, by-product of the fact that events happen in temporal sequence, and so does language, with a natural correlation following from that fact.

Serial order becomes a matter of syntactic interest when it is ARBITRARY, that is, (1) when a change from one order to another would produce a change of meaning that cannot be explained by a natural correlation with the order of events, or (2) when some serial order of words is disallowed by the language. The first is interesting because the grammar must explain how different orders correlate with different meanings. The second is interesting because the grammar must provide syntactic rules which assign, in some natural way, only the acceptable orders while disallowing the unacceptable ones.

Two kinds of order relationships play a significant role in natural languages: **adjacency** of words to one another, and **precedence** (i.e., one word precedes another). In adjacency relationships, it does not matter which of a pair of words precedes so long as they are next to each other (or as close as other considerations permit). In precedence relationships, it matters crucially whether one word precedes or follows another. Both relationships are conspicuous in Spanish:

> *El   presidente   es   un   pobre   hombre.*
> the   president   is   a   poor   man
> The president is a wretched man.
> (*poor* in the sense of deserving sympathy)

> *El   presidente   es   un   hombre   pobre.*
> the   president   is   a   man   poor
> The president is a poor man.
> (*poor* in the sense of lacking money)

In both sentences the adjacency relationship—the fact that the adjective *pobre* is next to the noun *hombre*—guarantees that the adjective will be understood as a modifier of *hombre*, not of some other word such as *presidente*. However, the precedence relationship is the reason that *pobre* is to be understood as 'wretched, deserving sympathy' in the first sentence but 'lacking money' in the second. Adjectives in Spanish are more likely to be taken in their literal sense when they follow a noun, but in a metaphorical sense when they precede it:

> *ideas diferentes* = differing (dissimilar) ideas
> ideas different
>
> *diferentes ideas* = various ideas

The 'adjacency' principle was perhaps best formulated by Otto Behaghel in his *Deutsche Syntax;* the principle (his first law) states that what belongs together semantically is placed together syntactically. All syntactic systems tend to provide juxtaposition or adjacency of related elements in linear strings, and to shun discontinuity. They tend to avoid allowing anything to stand between words that are semantically close. There are several principles which can override this one, so it has to be stated with the usual qualification: ALL OTHER THINGS BEING EQUAL, it is a valid principle. Two principles which can override it are (1) the HEAVIER ELEMENT PRINCIPLE: longer, heavier elements tend to come toward the end of sentences; and (2) the TOPICALIZATION PRINCIPLE: sentence elements that take up previously mentioned material tend to come before those that introduce new material.

The 'heavier element' principle is the basis for an important set of transformational rules called **extraposition** rules (Chapter VI). They provide, among other things, for the placement of heavy subjects (e.g., nominalized sentences) after the verb:

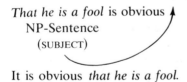

> *That he is a fool* is obvious
> NP-Sentence
> (SUBJECT)
>
> It is obvious *that he is a fool.*

The same principle explains the shifting of direct objects into final position whereas they would normally follow the verb immediately:

> He explained *the answer* to Mary yesterday.
>   NP
>   (DIRECT OBJECT)

He explained to Mary yesterday *that he would be late for the meeting.*
NP-Sentence
(DIRECT OBJECT)

The 'topicalization' principle is Behaghel's second law: the sentence element that is the subject of discussion, the **topic** of that part of the discourse—either because it has been mentioned previously or because it is conspicuous in the environment—tends to come first and to be destressed (downgraded by intonation or even reduced to some substitute form such as pronoun) in subsequent references to it, whereas the new information, the **comment**, tends to come near the end and to be highlighted by intonation. This principle rarely causes violations of the adjacency principle in the way that the heavier element principle regularly does. But when objects are topicalized, they are moved to the front, away from the verb to which they should be close, under the adjacency principle:

I like *cigarettes*—but cigars are too strong.
V   NP
(OBJECT)

Cigarettes I like, but cigars are too strong.

I like to own *Siamese cats especially,* but any cat is welcome here.
NP
(OBJECT)

Siamese cats especially I like to own, but any cat is welcome here.

Order of Main Sentence Elements

In the languages of the world there are three common serial orders among the main sentence elements in active declarative sentences (i.e., 'atomic' sentences). The main sentence elements are the SUBJECT-NP, the VERB, and the DIRECT-OBJECT-NP (often called the ACCUSATIVE OBJECT, from the name of the case that this object takes in Latin). Abbreviating these as S, V, and O, respectively, and taking the position of the verb as our criterion for classification, English order can be characterized as

verb-medial:

S	V	O
John	plays	the harpsichord.
All the children	expect	Christmas presents.
Dishonesty	begets	dishonesty.
John	believes	that he is right.

Japanese order is **verb-final**:

⏜S⏜		⏜O⏜		V
Neko	*ga*	*nezumi*	*o*	*toraeru.*
cat	SUBJECT	mouse	OBJECT	catches
	MARKER		MARKER	

The cat catches the mouse.

John	*wa*	*Mary*	*ni*	*au*	*daro.*
John	SUBJECT	Mary	OBJECT	see	will
	MARKER		MARKER		

John will see Mary.

Tagalog order is **verb-initial**, with some slight preference for subject-final (VOS), but most verb-initial languages are object-final (i.e., VSO):

V	S	O
Sumagot	*siya*	*sa propesor.*
answered	he	to-professor

He answered the professor.

V	O	S
Sumagot	*sa propesor*	*ang istudiante.*
answered	to-professor	the student

The student answered the professor.

   In many languages, including Old English and several other Germanic languages, both verb-medial and verb-final arrangements occur; in Modern German, the order in embedded sentences (subordinate clauses) is verb-final, but in the highest sentence (main clause), the order is verb-second. 'Verb-second' is a classification distinct from 'verb-medial', because in verb-medial languages like Modern English, the subject-NP must (in declarative sentences) precede the verb. In verb-second languages like German, SOME element must precede the verb, ONLY ONE element is permitted to precede the verb, and that element can be either the subject-NP or any of the complements attached to the verb. Furthermore, if the verb is itself complex (has one or more auxiliaries), only the finite verb—the form marked for tense—appears in second position, the rest remaining at the end of the clause as in the verb-final pattern:

GERMAN SUBORDINATE CLAUSE:　Verb-final

...(*weil*)　*die　Katze　die　Maus　gefangen　hat*
because　the　cat　　the　mouse　caught　has
...because the cat has caught the mouse

...(*weil*)　*Hans　Maria　gesehen　hat*
because　John　Mary　seen　　has
...because John has seen Mary

To convert a subordinate clause into a main clause (verb-second), delete the initial conjunction and move the finite verb to second position, as indicated by the arrows. Notice that German, on the basis of the second example, cannot be called either 'verb-medial' or 'verb-final', since the main clause declarative order has BOTH verb-medial and verb-final properties:

S　　　V　　　O　　　V
Hans　hat　Maria　gesehen.
　　　MEDIAL　　　　FINAL

This becomes even clearer with an example where there are several complements, ANY ONE of which can occur in the position before the finite verb:

SUBORDINATE ORDER

SUBJ　1-COMP　　2-COMP　　　3-COMP　　4-COMP

(*weil*) *Maria gestern auf dem Balkon ihrem neuen Freund das Buch gegeben haben muss*
Mary yesterday on-the-balcony to-her-new-friend the-book given　have　must
Mary must have given the book to her new friend on the balcony yesterday.

POSSIBLE MAIN ORDERS
SUBJ
(1) **Maria** *muss* 1-COMP 2-COMP 3-COMP 4-COMP *gegeben haben.*

1-COMP
(2) **Gestern** *muss* Maria 2-COMP 3-COMP 4-COMP *gegeben haben.*

2-COMP
(3) **Auf dem Balkon** *muss* Maria 1-COMP 3-COMP 4-COMP *gegeben haben.*

3-COMP
(4) **Ihrem neuen Freund** *muss* Maria 1-COMP 2-COMP 4-COMP *gegeben haben.*

4-COMP
(5) **Das Buch** *muss* Maria 1-COMP 2-COMP 3-COMP *gegeben haben.*

Schematically, the possibilities look like this:

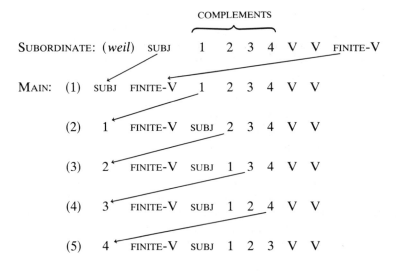

There are, then, four main serial-ordering arrangements of the main elements S, V, and O in declarative clauses:

1. Verb-medial: SVO
   e.g., English

2. Verb-final: SOV
   e.g., Japanese

3. Verb-initial: V $\begin{cases} SO \\ OS \end{cases}$
   e.g., Tagalog

4. Verb-second: XVX(V) = TVX (discussed below)
   e.g., German

The fourth one is easier to relate to the others if we note that the element which is immediately before the verb is the 'topic': symbolizing it with T, we can call the verb-second type TVX, with X representing whatever remains to the right of the finite verb.[1]

---

[1] Following here the usage of Theo Vennemann; the label 'verb-second' is, however, familiar in traditional grammatical literature and is perhaps to be preferred. But it requires the parallel usage of 'verb-initial', 'verb-medial', and 'verb-final', whereas the labels VSO, SVO, and SOV are more common.

The Importance of Verb–Object Order

The observations about the order of main elements in declarative clauses tell us very little about the role of serial-order rules in the syntax of natural languages until we add to them a further observation: The order of V and its accusative object is paralleled by a corresponding order in numerous other pairs of elements in the language.[2] For instance, if the basic order is VO, as in English, then the language will have PREpositions and not POSTpositions. If it is OV, as in Japanese, then the language will have POSTpositions and not PREpositions:

English: I went **to** Tokyo **by** train last week.

Japanese: *Watakushi*   *wa*   *senshū*   *densha de*   *Tōkyō e*   *itta.*
            I   SUBJ   last week   train-by   Tokyo-to   went

Recall, now, that in Chapter II we claimed that adpositions are predicates, like verbs. If the basic order of verbs and objects is VO, we would expect adpositions, being verblike in their semantic aspect, to follow the same order: PREP–OBJECT. If the basic order is OV, we would expect the reverse: OBJECT–POST, as it is in Japanese.

This observation can be extended further. In Chapter II we noted the difference between one-place predicates ('intransitive') and two-place predicates ('transitive'). We now want to think of the object-NP's of transitive predications as **modifiers** of the verb in the sense that they

---

[2] This observation is due to Joseph Greenberg (1963), in a brilliant study of some thirty languages. This work catapulted the study of questions of serial order and linguistic universals into a new prominence after years of neglect. The principle stated here, and the particular form of the subsequent presentation, are due to Bartsch and Vennemann (1972).

narrow down the meaning of the activity specified by the verb:

John left.
versus

John left $\begin{cases} \text{Mary.} \\ \text{his job.} \\ \text{the apartment.} \\ \text{no will.} \\ \ldots \end{cases}$

It is not conventional in syntactic theory to think of objects as modifiers, but doing so will give us a basis for making a generalization about serial order in a variety of languages: namely, that the order of all types of modifiers in relation to their **heads** (the words they modify) follows the same order as that of the verb and its object.[3]

This is a useful observation, if we consider the situation of the child trying to acquire his language; it would certainly not be reasonable to suppose that he has to master, one by one, an arbitrary serial order for any two elements that can occur in his language. If there is a system to it, all he needs is a key to the system and he will make the correct applications. The key appears to be that the serial order of 'head' and 'modifier' is relatively consistent for any language, and the position of the verb relative to its object is the most obvious clue to the typical order for that language. In perfectly consistent OV and VO languages, the regular orders are outlined in Table 1.

In a verb-second language like German, which is probably to be understood as an originally verb-final (OV) language in the process of changing to verb-medial (VO)—exactly as English has done in the last 1000 years—it is to be expected that some of its present serial ordering will be retained from its earlier OV form, while other structures will have changed to VO serialization. English, for example, preserves adjectives in front of nouns (from its earlier OV form), whereas Spanish, which has gone through the same kinds of serial-order change from OV to VO, preserves only a small set of prenominal adjectives, all with special meanings in that position. All others follow the noun—i.e., have changed to conform to the new head–modifier VO pattern.

For at least part of the regularity of this pattern, there is an explanation[4] that seems, in a common-sense way, to be persuasive. Forgetting about subjects for a moment, consider OV and VO as closely unified constructions. The language will resist anything being inserted

---

[3] This is 'the principle of natural serialization' of Bartsch and Vennemann (1972).

[4] Due originally to W. P. Lehmann.

TABLE 1

VO LANGUAGES		OV LANGUAGES	
(HEAD)	(MODIFIER)	(MODIFIER)	(HEAD)
1	2	1	2
1. Verb	Object	Object	Verb
2. Verb	Adverb	Adverb	Verb
3. Intensional Verb (*hope, believe*)	Infinitive	Infinitive	Intensional Verb
4. Modal Auxiliary (*can, must*)	Infinitive	Infinitive	Modal Auxiliary
5. Aspect, Tense (*is, did*)	Infinitive	Infinitive	Aspect, Tense
6. Auxiliary (*have*)	Participle	Participle	Auxiliary
7. Noun (English is aberrant; Spanish follows correctly.)	Adjective	Adjective	Noun
8. Noun	Relative Clause	Relative Clause	Noun
9. Noun (English: *book of John's;* the preposed genitive, *John's book*, is aberrant.)	Genitive (possessive)	Genitive	Noun
10. Comparative (*taller*)	Standard (*than Bill*)	Standard	Comparative
11. Preposition	NP	NP	Postposition

between the two elements of the construction. It follows, then, that if there is to be a modifier of the object, it will go on the left side in OV, on the right side in VO, since it must be adjacent to the head if possible (Behaghel's first law), and if placed on the other side it would interrupt the OV/VO unity:

(Noun-modifier)   OV
           VO   (Noun-modifier)

If there is to be a modifier of the verb, it will, by the same reasoning, go on the right side in OV and on the left side in VO:

           OV   (Verb-modifier)
(Verb-modifier)   VO

This is not sufficient to explain ALL the correlated facts about word order, but it does explain most of them.

Other Functions of Serial Order

Besides the head–modifier relationship which is signaled by one of the possible serial orders in a vast number of languages (including those where the relationship may also be marked by, for example, agreement rules of some kind), there are other semantic consequences of serial order. One of these is a direct function of Behaghel's second law, that topics precede comments in sentences. Since topics tend to be 'definite' by virtue of common focus, and since topics come early in sentences, there is a strong correlation between early position and definiteness. In Chinese, this correlation is exploited in the following way (tone marks omitted):

N V
Zei *pao* *le.*
thief run ASPECT
The thief has run away.

V   N
Pao *le*   *zei.*
run ASPECT thief
There escaped *a* thief.

     V
SUBJ ⌒⌒⌒ OBJECT
Haizi *dei* *lao* *yifu.*
child must iron clothes
The child has to iron (*some*) clothes.

       V
OBJECT SUBJ ⌒⌒⌒
Yifu *haizi* *dei* *lao.*
clothes child must iron
The child has to iron *the* clothes.

That is, position after the verb marks indefiniteness (unless a deictic—*this, that*—is used); position before the verb marks definiteness.

  A similar correlation is to be seen in English, though not so absolute. Predicate noun phrases—i.e., noun phrases after linking verbs like *be*—are almost invariably indefinite in English because they are the COMMENT part of such sentences, hence new information, not in common focus, not definite:

John is *a lawyer.*
*John is *the lawyer.*[5]

---

[5] This sentence is possible, or grammatical, only in a highly restricted context, e.g., *I have just mentioned a lawyer, a doctor, and a professor. John is the lawyer.* But in this context, *the lawyer* does not predicate anything about John; it merely identifies him.

The Poverty of Serial Order

As an information-carrying device, the serial order of words suffers from extreme poverty in the variety of distinctions it can make, even though it is of fundamental importance in all syntactic systems. It provides, after all, for only three possibilities, given that words occur one after another. (1) Two words can be close together in a sequence, or not. (2) The closest they can be is consecutive. (3) If consecutive, they can be in the order A followed by B, or B followed by A. Therefore serial order must be supplemented by other devices. The two main supplements are **morphology** and **intonation**.

Morphology

It is common to speak of linguistic structure as having two aspects, **syntagmatic** structure and **paradigmatic** structure. Syntagmatic structure is linear grouping provided by intonation, agreement, category selection/government, and serial-order constraints. Paradigmatic structure is not directly observable in any single sentence; it becomes apparent only upon comparison of the forms of words in two or more sentences. A **paradigm** for a word is constructed by listing the alternative forms of that word that appear in distinct functions.

In Old English, for example, the deictic word which corresponds to Modern English *that* had a rich set of distinct forms, depending on three parameters: (1) **number** (singular/plural), (2) **gender** (masculine/feminine/neuter), and (3) **case** distinctions between nominative (subject)/genitive (possessive)/dative (indirect object, approximately)/accusative (direct object)/instrumental (various adverbial functions). Thus there were $2 \times 3 \times 5$ (two numbers, three genders, five cases) distinct forms, ideally, in the paradigm:

	SINGULAR		
	MASC	FEM	NEUT
NOM	sē	sēo	þæt
GEN	þæs	þǣre	þæs
DAT	þǣm	þǣre	þǣm
ACCUS	þone	þā	þæt
INSTR	þȳ	þǣre	þȳ

ALL GENDERS PLURAL

NOM	p̄ā
GEN	p̄āra
DAT	p̄ǣm
ACCUS	p̄ā
INSTR	p̄ǣm

It is apparent at a glance that the full paradigm of thirty potentially distinct forms was not realized. All gender distinctions were collapsed in the plural; all but one of the plural forms were identical with some singular form; the only place where five case distinctions were realized was the masculine singular; there were only three distinct forms in the feminine singular, four in the neuter singular—but they were like the masculine singular except in one form. So the total number of distinct forms was nine in the singular, plus one more form distinct from any of these in the plural.

This is not an uncommon situation in natural languages. When words are **inflected** (modified in form, often by affixation) for such semantic features as number, gender, case, tense, and aspect, the inflections are rarely completely distinctive for all possible categories. Through long periods of time, sound change tends to grind away inflections, especially suffixes. There is a probably universal tendency for words to become shorter. This tendency is always thwarted by the necessity to communicate clearly. When the phonetic process of grinding down the length of words goes too far, new longer words are built up by compounding and word-formation processes of various types, and the cycle continues.

So long as the paradigmatic devices are unambiguous in determining relations between words in sentences—telling which word is subject, which is object, who did what to whom, and so on—then syntagmatic devices like serial ordering are less important for that language. Whenever the paradigmatic devices fail (as they invariably do, sooner or later), then syntagmatic devices take over. There are no languages in which devices of both types are not utilized; the differences are in the relative weight given to them at a particular time in the history of a particular language.

Morphology, the study and description of the forms of words, is traditionally divided into **derivational** morphology and **inflectional** morphology. The latter is concerned with those changes in the form of words which bear directly on their syntactic function in sentences, involving agreement, selection, and case-marking. The former is concerned with changes in the form of words which have the effect of creating new words, words that are distinct from the parent in ways other than those affecting syntactic relations. Typically, the words in these sets would be said to be derivationally related:

stable	phrase	sane	continue
stability	phrasal	sanity	continuity
establish	paraphrase	insane	continuation
establishment	paraphrastic	insanity	
stabilize		sanitary	
		sanitation	

necessary	doubt	note	combine (V)
necessity	dubious	notorious	combination
unnecessary	undoubtedly	notoriety	combinatory
necessitate	doubtlessly	notable	combine (N)
necessitation		noteworthy	
		notation	

It is apparent that the line between inflectional and derivational morphology is not a clean one. Derivational distinctions can sometimes be arranged in paradigms which have regular syntactic consequences:

The enemy *destroyed* the city.   V
The enemy's *destruction* of the city ...   N

The president *proposed* a solution.   V
The president's *proposal* of a solution ...   N

A solution is *necessary.*   ADJ
The *necessity* of a solution ...   N

I don't *doubt* whether he is *sane.*   V ... ADJ
I am not *dubious* about his *sanity.*   ADJ ... N

The most conspicuous difference between inflectional and derivational morphology is the relative generality and regularity of the former, as compared with the idiosyncrasy and capriciousness of the latter. An inflectional suffix like the English possessive '*s* can be attached to every animate noun, most inanimates, and even to whole phrases:

I accepted
⎧ the boy's apology.
⎪ the president's version.
⎨ the bank's foreclosure.
⎪ the book's title.
⎪ the pool's cost.
⎩ the King of England's resignation.

But derivational affixes do not go across the board this way:

sane	smart	intelligent	
sanity	*smartity	*intelligentity	

propose	refuse	deny	demolish
proposal	refusal	denial	*demolishal
proposition	*refusition	*denition	demolition

compare	repair	compose	repose
comparison	*repairison	composition	*reposition

For this reason many linguists consider derivational aspects of words to be simply a part of the lexicon, the dictionary, of the language, not a part of the syntax, even though a total description of a language's structure must extract as much regularity as possible from the derivational processes of word formation. Inflectional morphology, on the other hand, is a central focus of any syntactic description, because inflectional processes are general and directly functional in determining relations between words in sentence formation. To put it another way, inflectional processes, though they change the forms of words, are part of the process of SENTENCE formation; derivational processes, though they change the forms of sentences, are part of the process of WORD formation. Derivational affixes are additional content elements, with meanings like 'an abstract entity notion corresponding to a particular action predicate', as in *persevere/perseverance;* or 'an individual who regularly performs the action of a particular predicate', as in *work/worker;* or 'a condition of mind corresponding to a particular predicate', as in *doubt/dubious;* or 'a state predicate about existence of the corresponding entity', as in *malice/ malicious.*

Inflectional systems range, in languages of the world, from extremely rich (e.g., Finnish, Tagalog, Sanskrit) to relatively poor (e.g., Chinese, English). For an inflectional system to be a good communicative device, the inflectional affixes must be CONSPICUOUS, UNIFORM, and RELIABLE. The Old English forms of the word *that* listed above were not reliable, because, for example, *þā* could mean either feminine accusative singular or nominative/accusative plural; *þǣre* could mean feminine genitive, dative, or instrumental singular—and so on. They also were not uniform: the nominative masculine and feminine forms *sē* and *sēo* began with the sound *s-,* though all the others began with *þ-.* Compared with most other characteristics of the Old English inflectional system, they were at least fairly conspicuous. But look at some forms of the Old

English personal pronouns:

hē   hēo   hīe
he   she   they

The differences between these are quite inconspicuous. It is no wonder that two of the three modern forms (*she* and *they*) had to be borrowed from the tongue of the Norse invaders at an early date.

It is clear that inflectional systems are potentially much richer devices than serial-order systems. There is no limit to the extent of semantic information that can, in principle, be conveyed in this way. But it is also a fact that many languages get along with very little inflection. There appears to be no 'optimal' balance between the two, though there does seem to be a cycle of change by which inflectional systems become cumbersome, collapse in part, perhaps thereby bringing about changes in the importance of serial-order information, then develop new inflections (e.g., from prepositions or postpositions), and cycle again.

Intonation

This second device to enrich the fundamental but impoverished capability of serial word-order distinctions is given too little credit in most grammars because they tend to deal with language on paper, where it is inconvenient to mark phonetic features that are matters of pitch and rhythm. Indeed, many examples that are taken as ambiguous would never in fact be ambiguous in real speech. Examples like the following:

Computers are manufacturing tools.

Mary and Jane are visiting relatives.

The wives all tried sewing circles.

He tried to get the lamb to turn on the rotisserie.

can all be disambiguated by intonation simply by rhythmically grouping either of the pairs indicated by braces. A major semantic distinction in

English, namely that between 'restrictive' relative clauses and 'nonrestrictive' (or 'appositive') clauses depends, in many clear cases, ENTIRELY on
intonation, marked by commas in standard orthography:

RESTRICTIVE
> The children who knew how to swim were permitted to ride in
> the boat without life jackets.
> (But the ones who didn't know how had to wear them.)

APPOSITIVE
> The children, who knew how to swim, were permitted to ride in
> the boat without life jackets.
> (All of them had this privilege because of their knowledge.)

In sentences where an incorrect perception of the word clusters would
lead to misunderstanding, intonational flagging of boundaries is
obligatory:

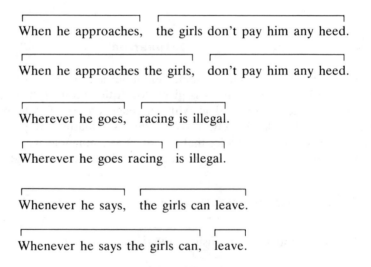

But of course such trick examples are rare; most of the time,
intonation is used to REINFORCE the grouping of words into semantically
related and functional clusters that are suggested by word order, morphology, and category selection/government. This kind of reinforcement
is obvious in the perception of main sentence elements like subject and
predicate in SVO languages, where any subject of some weight (i.e., not
merely a pronoun or short NP) will tend to occur in an intonational unit

separate from the intonational unit that holds the predicate together:

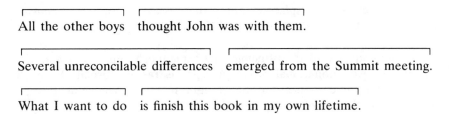

All the other boys   thought John was with them.

Several unreconcilable differences   emerged from the Summit meeting.

What I want to do   is finish this book in my own lifetime.

In a wide variety of languages there is one function that is, if not uniquely that of intonation, certainly served primarily by intonation and only secondarily by other syntactic devices. This is comment marking (and, by inference, also topic marking). If a sentence is a breath group— i.e., spoken entirely in a single exhalation—the 'natural' intonation should be a steady fall in pitch from beginning to end, since there is a one-to-one correlation between greater air pressure and higher pitch in speech production. But there is also a syntactic principle which places material from previous context early in the sentence, with new information toward the end (Behaghel's second law). A second syntactic principle, the **contrastive prominence** principle, calls for the highlighting of contrasted information (information that is paired into opposites: *I said A, not B*). These two principles are probably to be understood as a single general principle which says: WHATEVER IS MOST IMPORTANT SEMANTICALLY SHOULD SOUND MOST PROMINENT INTONATIONALLY. The principle is very clear in these examples:

One of their sons is a doctor in *Los Angeles*, and the other practices medicine in *New York.*
(Both are doctors, and the contrast is between the two locations.)

One of their sons is a *doctor* in *Los Angeles*, and the other practices *law* in *New York.*
(One is a doctor, the other a lawyer; there are two contrasts: one between *doctor* and *lawyer*, the other between *Los Angeles* and *New York.*)

Elizabeth is the Queen of *England*, and Juliana the Queen of *Holland.*
(Both are queens: contrast between their countries.)

Johnson was *vice*-president of the United States before he became *president.*
(Contrast between *vice-president* and, as it were, *full president.*)

First they assassinated *John* Kennedy, *then* they assassinated *Bobby*.
(Notice how strange it would sound if the intonational prominence were misplaced: **First* they assassinated John *Kennedy,
then* they assassinated Bobby *Kennedy*.)

The converse of the principle that semantically important material
should receive intonational prominence is **destressing** (usually by pitch
lowering) of parenthetical or low-content material. We show this by
reduced type in the following example:

All the King's men—they were lousy mechanics anyway—couldn't
put Humpty together again.

Since anaphoric material—material of which the reference is understood
from previous mention or common focus—is by definition NOT new
information, it is regularly destressed, like the word *so* below:

Is John *leaving*? I don't *think* so.
(Notice how strange it would sound, since *so* is anaphoric, to say,
I don't think SO.)

The anaphoric destressing principle is overridden by the contrastive
prominence principle:

John called Mary a *Democrat*, and then *she* insulted *him*.
John called Mary a *Democrat*, and then she *insulted* him.

In the first of these examples, it is presupposed that being called a
Democrat is insulting; otherwise *insulted* could not be destressed (since it
would not be anaphoric). In the second example, no such presupposition
exists, and the pronouns *she* and *him* are destressed, being anaphoric,
and the new content (*insulted*) receives the major intonational prominence.

Intonation, like word order, is a relatively poor device. It is capable
of providing for only three coding functions: (1) a **separational** function,
by rhythmic spacing of words into clusters; (2) a **focusing** function, by
attaching pitch prominence to semantically important material, and by
destressing anaphoric material; and (3) an **identifying** function, by assignment of special contours (e.g., rising) to special sentence types like
questions. It is not surprising that most of its functions are duplicated by
other devices such as serial word-order or morphological agreement or
specially marked constructions (e.g., for *JOHN left early*, English has
constructions like *It was JOHN who left early* or *JOHN was the one who*

left early). Languages rarely allow a significant distinction to be symbolized by only one device. They tend to be redundant, to provide ample insurance that what is not understood from one clue will be picked up from another.

Signals Grammar

In the history of syntactic study, there have been times when virtually all the emphasis was on the description of the 'signals' that hearers use to 'decode the message' contained in a sentence—'signals' meaning the four devices discussed in this chapter (serial order, morphology, intonation, and category membership), 'decode the message' meaning to discover the speaker's intended semantic interpretation. This particular aspect of syntactic study, after being out of fashion for a while, has achieved new prominence under such names as 'perceptual strategies' in recent years. It is important not to lose sight of the information that is directly available through these signals, but the modern revolution in the study of syntax came when attention was directed away from these surface properties toward more abstract characteristics of syntactic relations which had been neglected, to a large extent, by the linguistic theories that went before. We turn now to these more abstract characteristics.

Constituent Structure

In Chapter III we examined the variety of coding devices that are directly observable on the surface of sentences for signaling syntactic information: information about the organization of sentences, the relations of parts to each other, information that enables a speaker/hearer to construct semantic interpretations. In Chapter I we saw that what is known about semantic interpretation clearly requires that sentences be understood as having **hierarchical** organization. Such organization can be efficiently represented with branching diagrams either above or below the words, with syntactic category labels at the nodes where the branches intersect.

These branching diagrams have been referred to by various names in the syntactic literature. Perhaps the most widely familiar name for them is **phrase-marker** (P-marker, for short), following Noam Chomsky's usage. They represent the organization of the sentence into a hierarchy of units (**constituents**—units out of which it is constituted). More informally, phrase-markers are referred to simply as syntactic **trees**, or **tree-diagrams**.

Tree-diagrams may be drawn to represent semantic and logical aspects of a sentence's organization, or they may be drawn directly over the linear string of words to represent syntactic grouping at the surface level, or they may be used to represent stages in between these two extremes. The most abstract tree is often referred to as the **Logical Form** or **Semantic Structure** of the sentence; the least abstract one is referred to as the **Surface Structure.** Intermediate structures between these extremes have been referred to by various names. If they are conceived as relatively closer to the Semantic Structure, the label **Deep Structure** has been used; if relatively closer to the Surface Structure, the label **Shallow Structure** has been suggested. For any given sentence, many different tree-diagrams can be drawn appropriately, depending on what one is trying to show about the sentence and about how it is interpreted. All such diagrams are like two-dimensional drawings of multidimensional space, whether an architect's blueprints or an artist's view of the finished project. They are meaningful only if one understands the conventions under which they are to be interpreted.

In what follows here, we shall set forth some aspects of tree-diagraming as applied to English. Diagrams appropriate to other languages will not be like those of English in detail. To the extent that serial order of words is different, for example, the organization of phrases from left to right in the diagrams is also necessarily different. All languages share many substantive syntactic characteristics ('syntactic universals'), but the details of constituent structure—which words cluster together in what order—are certainly not among them. What IS universal is that all languages have constituent structure of the same general type, that all languages display relational information in the Surface Structure by coding devices drawn from a small universal set (serial order, adpositions, morphological inflections, category differences, intonational phrasing), and that the Semantic Structures which these devices symbolize are the same across all languages (i.e., universal), or at least very similar.

All diagraming begins with the assumption that the category membership of words in a sentence is known. We may assume that it is in the lexicon, since it is certainly part of the tacit knowledge of any speaker of the language. This knowledge enables one to place labels like N, ADJ, V, ART, ADV, PREP, etc., above every word in the string. These category labels are the lowest-level constituents in the sentence.

The remaining steps in diagraming are repetitions of one single operation: DETERMINE WHICH CATEGORIES BELONG TOGETHER AS MEMBERS OF A LARGER UNIT. That larger unit is assigned a phrase (P) label which corresponds to the syntactic category label that belongs to the governing word, the 'head', of the cluster; e.g., above a phrase governed by an N, we assign NP; above one governed by a PREP, we assign PrepP; above one governed by a V, we assign VP; at the top we place S for 'sentence'. It is not always easy to determine which word is the governor in a phrase, and one must try to find persuasive reasons in support of one decision or another in particular cases. Some of the kinds of reasons that appear in the syntactic literature are illustrated below.

Consider this sentence:

> An effective dean can reverse an unwise departmental recommendation about tenure.

Assigning category labels, we have:

    ART   ADJ   N   V   V   ART ADJ   ADJ
    An effective dean can reverse an unwise departmental

       N   PREP   N
    recommendation about tenure.

In general, the head will be that word which cannot be deleted from the construction without destroying the syntactic relations within the sentence. It is the word within a phrase which governs the selection, and often the form, of the satellites in the phrase. Consider the first three words of the example:

    ART   ADJ   N
    an   effective dean

It is clear that *dean* is modified, limited in meaning, by the ADJ—it is not just ANY dean, but one who is effective. The ART *an*, in turn, further specifies that the *effective dean* is not a particular one who has been previously identified. It indicates, on the contrary, that we have in mind a TYPE of individual. To represent this information, a tree like this is called for:

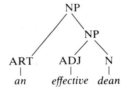

The same criteria will lead to an analysis of *an unwise departmental recommendation* like this:

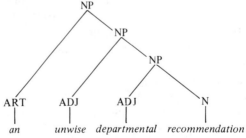

But we have left out *about tenure* in this analysis so far. Clearly it is a modifier of the noun *recommendation* in the same way that *departmental* is. The problem is, which of the NP nodes should it be attached to? Indeed, do we NEED all those nodes? There are several alternatives:

(1)

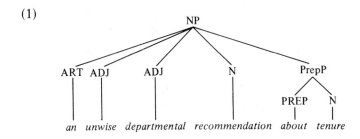

(2)

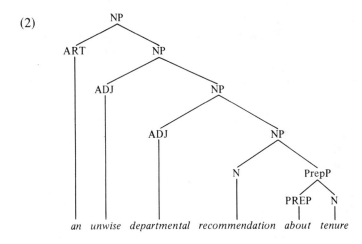

(3)

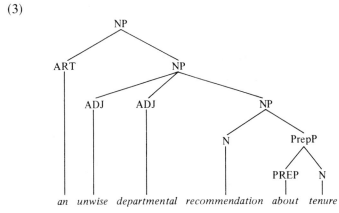

(4)

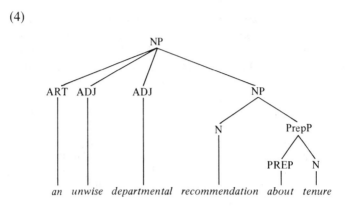

an   unwise   departmental   recommendation   about   tenure

How are these four different in their substantive claims—that is, how do the relations they represent differ in ways that will affect the semantic interpretation? All four trees claim that the whole string is a noun phrase—that is, the whole string is a phrasal unit which functions, in its semantic relation to the rest of the sentence, in whatever role is appropriate for noun phrases (subject, direct object, indirect object, object of preposition). All but (1) claim that *recommendation about tenure* is a subunit within the larger NP—i.e., that what was *departmental,* or what was *unwise,* was the *recommendation-about-tenure.* Tree (1), on the other hand, claims that *about tenure* is a modifying phrase exactly on a par with *unwise* and *departmental*; it is a recommendation which has three predicates concerning it—it was unwise, it was departmental, and it was about tenure. Tree (2) makes the most extensive claims of all; it claims that of all recommendations about tenure, there is a subset that can be called departmental; of that subset there is a further subset that can be called unwise. Thus (2) looks like this:

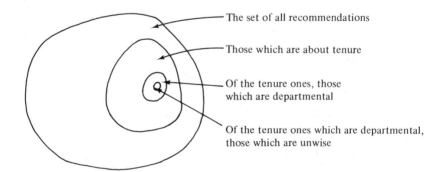

(1), on the other hand, looks like this:

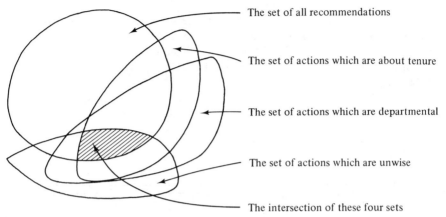

The set of all recommendations

The set of actions which are about tenure

The set of actions which are departmental

The set of actions which are unwise

The intersection of these four sets

Extensionally, in terms of the real world, there is no difference between (1) and (2). They refer to all and only the same events. Intensionally, in how we feel about the semantic relations, there is a difference. Grammarians have argued for both analyses.

Tree (2), in which each ADJ (and the ART) appears as a higher predicate, is probably a closer approximation to an adequate semantic representation. But each of these predicates, in an adequate representation of the semantics, would appear in a separate sentence structure of its own (they would be full relative clauses: *a recommendation—which was about tenure—which was departmental—which was unwise...*). Since it is necessary to construct such a semantic representation anyway, and since the Surface Structure is intended to represent only minimal information about the clustering of predicates and participants, most linguists would probably consider tree (1) to be an adequate diagram of the Surface Structure of the phrase. It is simpler in the sense that it makes fewer claims about the internal structure of the phrase; it has a 'flatter' configuration, which is generally assumed to be characteristic of Surface Structures.

In order to produce trees which normally have the flatter configuration of (1), the diagraming procedure must be revised to look for the head of EACH phrase (instead of grouping words in pairs) and to assign a label corresponding to the head ONCE ONLY for that phrase. Thus *an effective dean* would be assigned this structure:

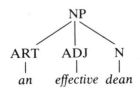

and *an unwise departmental recommendation about tenure* would have the structure shown as (1) above.

The only unanalyzed words left in the sentence are *can* and *reverse*. We saw earlier that the complements of verbs form a unit with the verb, such that a transitive verb with its object is equivalent in syntactic range to an intransitive verb. So we can attach the direct-object-NP to the verb to form a VP:

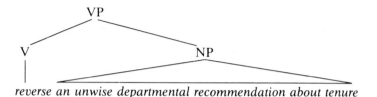

reverse an unwise departmental recommendation about tenure

Several kinds of evidence support this analysis of *reverse... tenure* as a single constituent. For instance, if we say, 'A dean can do many things: he can_____', the blank can be filled by such phrases as the following:

smile
quit
quit his job
fire professors
reverse recommendations

including, of course, the entire phrase *reverse... tenure* in the diagram above. The point is that whether these phrases are single-word intransitive verbs like *smile* or transitive verb phrases of any length, they are syntactically equivalent in relation to the modal auxiliary *can*. *Can* itself is also a verb, a special kind of verb (see Chapter II for a discussion of the AUX, in particular the modal), which takes the rest of the VP as its complement:

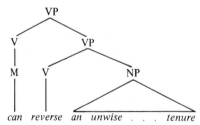

can reverse an unwise . . . tenure

Our diagram once again, as it did in our pairwise analysis of the NP earlier, is moving to considerable potential depth within the tree, so that if we have several auxiliary verbs, we get something like this:

(John) may have been drawing trees.

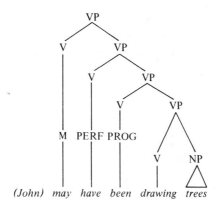

We need, somewhere in the grammar, a device which will disallow ungrammatical sequences of verbs like these:

    *have may be draw
    *will be have drawing
    *will drawing
    *have draw

This can be done rather simply by a syntactic feature that is attached, in the lexicon, to each auxiliary verb, e.g., a feature on *may* which says, in part, 'must be followed by a VP of which the first element is a V in its basic form (not V-*ing* or V-*ed*)'. We will return to such syntactic features in Chapter VI.

   Now we have reduced the string of eleven words to a string of two categories (using triangles to abbreviate the details of the branching diagrams):

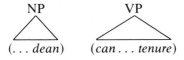

At this point we have run out of governing words to use as the basis for a still higher-node label. The relationship between the highest NP and the highest VP is unique. To it, we assign the label **sentence** (abbreviated S):

With everything filled in, the full tree looks like (5):

(5)

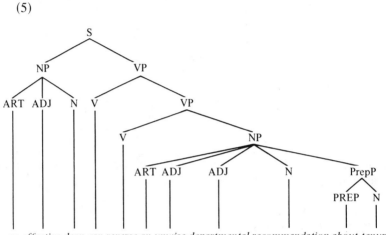

an effective dean can reverse an unwise departmental recommendation about tenure

---

Beyond Surface Structures

All sentences can be diagramed in this way, with labels and brackets assigned directly to the linear string of words to represent the surface organization of a sentence. However, the aim of such diagrams is to represent some basic information about the hierarchical relations that determine part of the meaning of the sentence. If we have a pair (or more) of sentence types that are understood in the same way, although their surface diagrams are different, we must try to find some level of representation at which their similarity (or identity) is expressed. Consider a pair of sentences like these:

He looked up the answer.
He looked the answer up.

Because the position of *up* is different, they must be represented by two distinct surface diagrams:

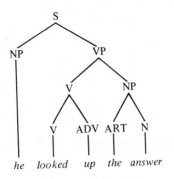

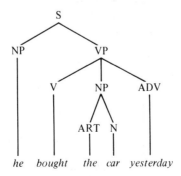

The second of these suggests that *up* is an adverb related to the verb somewhat like *yesterday* in *He bought the car yesterday,* or like *thoughtfully* in *He considered the question thoughtfully:*

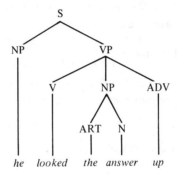

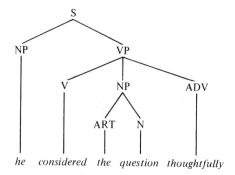

But this apparent similarity is misleading. Both *yesterday* and *thoughtfully* are predicates over actions or events:

His buying of the car *occurred yesterday.*
His consideration of the question *was thoughtful.*

But *up* is not a predicate at all:

*His looking of the answer $\begin{cases} was\ up. \\ occurred\ up. \end{cases}$

Only the first of the two trees for *look up* shows it to be a unit, equivalent to *find* or *discover* or *research* as a lexical unit:

He $\begin{cases} \text{looked up} \\ \text{found} \\ \text{discovered} \\ \text{researched} \end{cases}$ the answer.

Apparently *He looked the answer up* cannot be assigned a diagram by the kind of direct analysis of a linear string that we saw earlier, at least not one which reveals very much about the Semantic Structure of the sentence. Rather, it needs to be diagramed at a slightly more abstract level, where *look . . . up* is a single lexical unit:

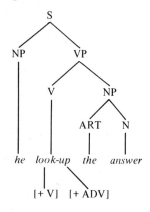

In this diagram, the LEXICAL information that *look-up* is a unit is reflected by the fact that it appears like any other verb under a single node V. The syntactic information that this lexical item consists of a sequence of two categories, V and ADV, is shown in square brackets under the entry. This diagram may be thought of as underlying both *He looked up the answer* and *He looked the answer up*. To relate the abstract diagram to the first of these sentences, nothing is required except to project up into the diagram the features given in square brackets. To relate the diagram to the second sentence, something more complex needs doing. A rule which moves *up* from one position to another must apply:

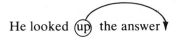

He looked (up) the answer

Such a **movement rule** has no function except to provide, from a single abstract diagram, the two distinct serial orders in which these words can be arranged. But given rules of this type, we can invent diagrams for sets of semantically similar sentences which will directly reveal those similarities. We will feel free, then, to try to invent such diagrams in general, since the hierarchical structures which we invent have no value for the study of syntax except for the light that they throw on semantic interpretation.

Diagrams: Surface vs. Abstract

Abstract diagrams of sentences may differ from surface diagrams in several ways. The differences that show up most frequently are summarized below. These differences are to be understood as having semantically minimal consequences. They may reflect differences in emphasis or focus, but not the basic meaning of the sentences.

1. The same units may appear in different serial orders (with correspondingly different diagrams):

> He looked up the answer.
> He looked the answer up.
>
> He solved the problem easily.
> He easily solved the problem.

2. Differences in serial order may be accompanied by special forms that code certain functions. We may consider them to be **tracer** elements associated with those constructions (see item 4 below):

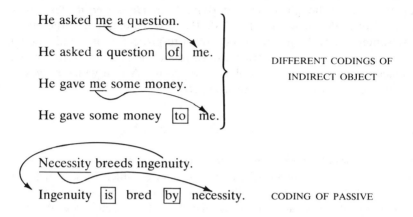

He asked me a question.

He asked a question of me.

He gave me some money.

He gave some money to me.

DIFFERENT CODINGS OF
INDIRECT OBJECT

Necessity breeds ingenuity.

Ingenuity is bred by necessity.   CODING OF PASSIVE

3. The more abstract diagram may contain elements that are absent from the surface (they are understood to be present in the meaning, and are therefore explicitly included in the diagram that is closer to a representation of the meaning):

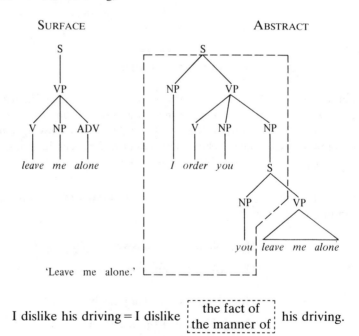

SURFACE   ABSTRACT

'Leave me alone.'

I dislike his driving = I dislike   the fact of / the manner of   his driving.

4. The surface diagram may contain elements that are absent from the more abstract diagram. These are tracer elements, affixes or words which are not meaningful in themselves except that they provide a way to trace the abstract semantic relationships which are not directly represented in the surface. They function to identify certain construction (as in 2 above), and to enable us to reconstruct a complex hierarchy from a linear string:

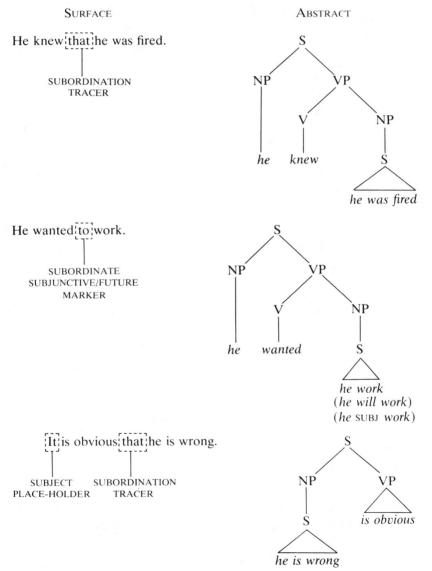

5. The syntactic category to which a word belongs on the surface may be different in the more abstract analysis:

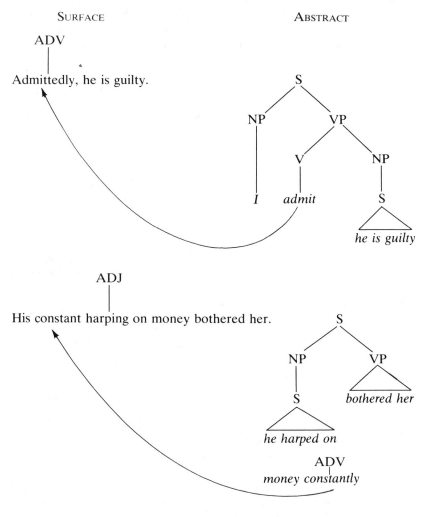

6. The surface may have substitute forms whose full forms (antecedents) appear in the abstract analysis:

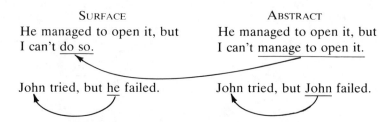

English Trees

It is not easy to acquire facility in drawing approximately accurate tree-diagrams for English sentences. Many books present rules for deriving trees starting from an initial node S. There is little difficulty in understanding how to carry out these instructions. The inverse of this task, namely, given a sentence, figure out what an appropriate diagram would be, is more difficult by several orders of magnitude. We present below these two tasks, (1) top-down derivation of sentences, and (2) bottom-up diagraming of sentences. The first task is done by following, quite mechanically, rules of the type shown below, which are called **constituent-structure** rules, or **phrase-structure** rules:

1. S → NP VP (ADV)

2. NP → $\begin{cases} \text{NP} & \text{S} \\ \text{DET N} & \text{(S)} \\ \text{S} \end{cases}$

3. VP → V $\left(\begin{Bmatrix} \begin{bmatrix} \text{NP} & \text{(NP)} \\ \text{VP} \\ \text{AP} \end{bmatrix} \end{Bmatrix} \right)$

4. AP → $\begin{cases} \text{ADJ} & \text{(S)} \\ \text{PrepP} \end{cases}$

5. DET → $\begin{Bmatrix} \text{ART} \\ \text{DEICTIC} \end{Bmatrix}$ (QUANT)

The arrow means, draw a tree in which the symbol at the left is placed above the symbol(s) at the right, and attach the right-hand symbols to it as lower branches. By convention, only one line of a set of elements in braces can be chosen, and elements in parentheses can be included or not. Thus application of rule 1 yields two trees:

Rule 2 yields four further possible branchings (only one being permitted from any single occurrence of NP):

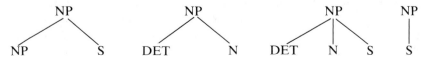

Rule 3 yields five more (again only one per VP):

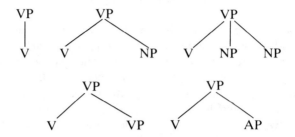

Rule 4 expands the AP to provide adjectival predicates with or without sentential complements, and a limited class of prepositional phrases (e.g., *The party is at nine o'clock; The book is on the table*):

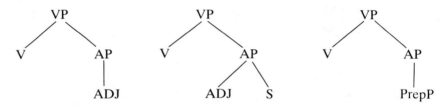

Rule 5 expands the determiner:

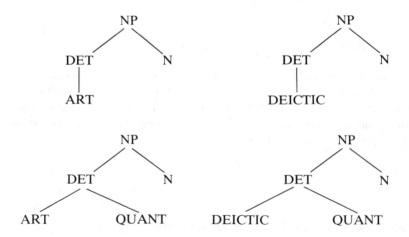

All the rules apply whenever a symbol on the left side of an arrow shows up in the tree. So if, in rule 2, we select the expansion on the first line of that rule, we must begin the derivation again for S (circled in the following tree):

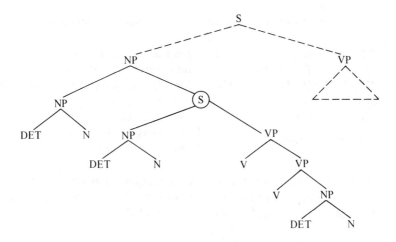

It is apparent that if we continue in this way, we will soon run out of pieces of paper large enough to write our diagram on. The clear fact is that although it is conventional to present derivations in this top-down fashion, no one ever, either in linguistics classes or in anything resembling the activity of speech, derives sentences in this way. What, therefore, is the CONTENT of such rules? That is, if we don't, even in the classroom, derive sentences this way, what is their value?

Their content is simply this: they provide a compact set of generalizations about the POSSIBLE phrase-structure systems in a language. They say explicitly that the internal structure of NP, for example, must be one of the trees characterized by the rules which follow NP → .... They provide an encapsulated view of a set of basic active declarative sentence diagrams, and they show those points at which sentences may be embedded to produce complex sentences (i.e., whenever S turns up in a rule).

Consider now the task which is closer to what linguists do, and much closer to what students of syntax must learn to do fluently: given a sentence, draw an abstract tree-diagram which fits it. The discussion below presents some strategies which make this a feasible task. It is relatively easy to draw a SURFACE diagram by following the steps outlined at the beginning of this chapter. Our discussion now has to do with strategies for determining one or more ABSTRACT diagrams, diagrams that are closer to the bases of semantic interpretation. We restrict our discussion to ENGLISH constituent structure, but the heuristic principles are universal.

In any language, the number of simple sentence types is very small. By 'simple sentence' we mean just those active declarative sentences containing only one finite verb (marked for tense) and no nonfinite verbs: 'atomic' or 'kernel' sentences. In English there are six of them (the number will vary from language to language, but only slightly):[1]

1. NP V (ADV)   John arrived (on Friday).
2. NP V NP (ADV)   John threw the ball (hard).
3. NP V NP NP (ADV)   John threw Mary the ball (angrily).
4. NP *be* NP   John is a lawyer.
5. NP *be* ADJ   John is intelligent.
6. NP *be* PrepP   ⎰ The party is at nine o'clock.
                             ⎱ The book is on the table.

As written above, the category strings are **sentence patterns**. A sentence pattern is determined by extracting nodes from left to right in a tree so that no element of the surface string is excluded:

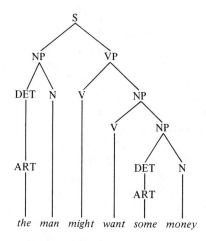

From this tree we can extract various sentence patterns, among which are these:

NP VP

DET N VP

NP V VP

DET N V V NP

ART N VP

ART N V V ART N

---

[1] The node ADV is provided optionally in these patterns. As we saw in Chapter II, there is considerable reason to believe that most adverbs do not in fact appear in sentences as part of the atomic core but rather are inserted from higher predicates, or from coordinate sentences.

In short, a sentence pattern is an abbreviation for a tree-diagram, at whatever level of abstraction is convenient for one's purposes.

By using parentheses and brace notation, the basic six sentence patterns of English can be further reduced to two formulas:

(1)   NP   V   (NP)   (NP)   (ADV) = 1, 2, 3 above

$$(2) \quad \text{NP} \quad be \quad \begin{Bmatrix} \text{NP} \\ \text{ADJ} \\ \text{PrepP} \end{Bmatrix} = 4, 5, 6 \text{ above}$$

Now, with these atomic sentence patterns in mind, along with the possible expansions of these nodes summarized by the phrase-structure rules given earlier, we can illustrate how complex sentences are abstractly diagramed. The essential notion is that for every verb in the sentence (except modal and aspectual verbs—i.e., auxiliaries—and even they belong to separate sentences in a more abstract analysis), there must be an atomic sentence, however much distorted on the surface, embedded somewhere in the full sentence. That embedded sentence itself will have the form of an atomic sentence in the abstract tree-diagram. The phrase-structure rules allow the node S to be introduced at only four points:

NP → NP   S   (Relative Clause)

NP → DET   N   S   (Noun Complement)

NP → S   (Noun Clause)

AP → ADJ   S   (Adjective Complement)

Consider noun clauses first:

Mary said she was leaving.

We note that there are two verbs, *said* and *was leaving*. There must be two atomic sentences. The verb *say* occurs in the pattern NP   V   NP (e.g., *Mary said something*). We therefore posit this phrase-marker:

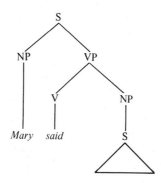

The structure of the lower S follows the NP VP atomic pattern:

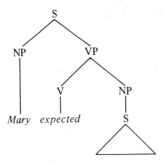

```
                    S
                  /   \
               NP      VP
                |     /  \
                |    V     NP
                |    |      |
             Mary  said     S
                         /    \
                       NP      VP
                        |     /  \
                        |    V    VP
                        |    |     |
                        |    |     V
                        |    |     |
                       she  was  leaving
                             [+ AUX]
```

Now, with another sentence, we add a slight additional complicating factor:

Mary expected to leave.

Again there are two verbs: *expect* and *leave*. There must be two S's in the tree. Since *expect* can take simple NP objects, we postulate again the NP V NP atomic pattern:

```
                    S
                  /   \
               NP      VP
                |     /  \
                |    V     NP
                |    |      |
             Mary expected  S
                           /_\
```

The embedded S, like every S, must have a subject (the first phrase-structure rule expands S into NP VP, i.e., subject – predicate). But there is no other NP after the verb *expect*. We therefore supply one from the semantics of the sentence: it means that Mary expected that she (Mary) would leave. (Cf. *Mary expected John to leave.*) Hence:

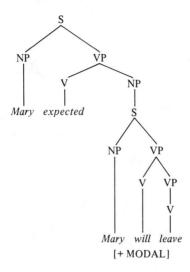

The word *to* does not emerge from ANY category in the phrase-structure rules; it must therefore be a tracer element inserted by rules we have not yet seen (Chapters V and VI) which take this abstract tree-diagram and convert it into a linear string. Those rules must delete the lower occurrence of *Mary* and replace the modal verb *will* with *to*, thereby producing the sentence *Mary expected to leave.*

Such rules seem like pure hocus-pocus at this point. But notice what they gain us, if we take them on faith for the moment. ALL declarative active sentences can be analyzed as having just the six atomic sentence patterns as their basic building blocks. These patterns appear over and over again, stacked in various hierarchies, and the fundamental syntactic relationships are still the ones represented in the atomic sentence patterns. The grotesque alternative would be to have huge numbers of phrase-structure rules to characterize directly all the possible mutations that emerge from this kind of hierarchical stacking of elementary kernels.

Consider now a fairly complex sentence:

The girl who lives next door persuaded two friends to help her paint the kitchen.

There are four verbs: *lives, persuaded, help, paint.* There must be four S's in the tree. *Lives* is transparently in a relative clause, and the main verb is *persuade. Persuade* is semantically a three-place predicate; i.e., *someone* (1) persuades *someone else* (2) of *something* (3). It therefore falls into the

NP V NP NP atomic pattern:

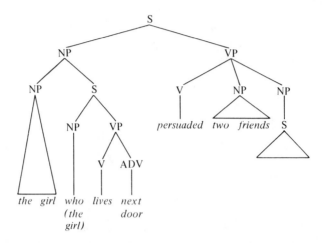

The S on the lower right-hand side of the tree must be complex itself, since it contains two verbs, *help* and *paint*. Like *persuade, help* is a three-place predicate; i.e., *someone* (1) helps *someone else* (2) in *some action* (3). So, abbreviating the above somewhat for clarity, we have:

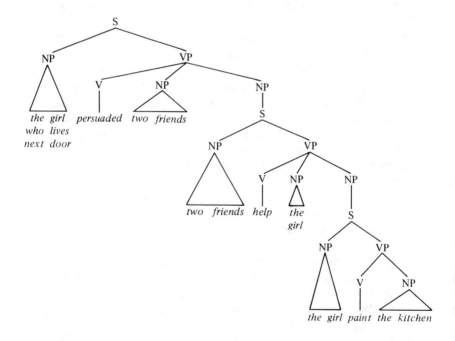

If we read this off from left to right, it doesn't sound much like an English sentence:

The girl—who lives next door—persuaded two friends—two friends help the girl—the girl paint the kitchen.

But if we substitute the pronouns *she/her* for *the girl* after the first occurrence, and delete the repetitions, inserting *to* judiciously under conditions that will be discussed in Chapter VII, we have the sentence we set out to analyze:

The girl who lives next door persuaded two friends ~~two friends~~ to help her ~~she~~ paint the kitchen.

Now consider one more example:

His failing the exam proved that he was wrong in deciding to quit school.

There are five verbs: *failing, proved, was (wrong), deciding, quit.* To find the main verb, we ask which ones are inflected for tense (PAST/PRESENT), which reduces the list of five to two, *proved* and *was wrong*. *Was wrong* is in a subordinate clause, marked by *that.* So there is only one possible candidate for main verb, namely *proved.* Its subject is a reduced noun clause (gerundive in form, for reasons that we discuss in Chapter VI):

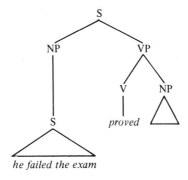

Since *proved* is a transitive verb (NP V NP), its object must be the noun clause beginning with *that*:

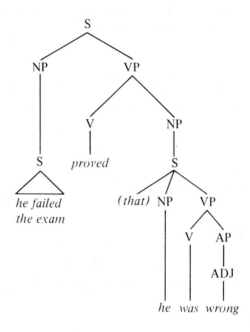

We still have two verbs unaccounted for, *deciding* and *quit.* What is the relation of the phrase *in deciding to quit* to its surface head, the adjective *wrong*? It is not adverbial, since it predicates nothing about his wrongness. Rather, wrongness is predicated about his decision:

> He was wrong in deciding to quit.
> = His deciding to quit was wrong.

With this clue, we can reconsider the structure of the noun clause *that he was wrong in deciding to quit school:*

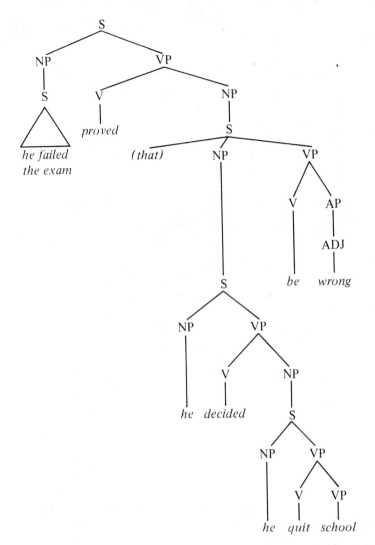

It is clear that it will take some remarkable rules to convert this structure into the sentence we started with, so remarkable, indeed, that many linguists would claim we have gone too far in abstractness, too far toward the Semantic Structure (how far one can or should go is by no means settled). If this is too far, the closer-to-surface structure can be accepted instead:

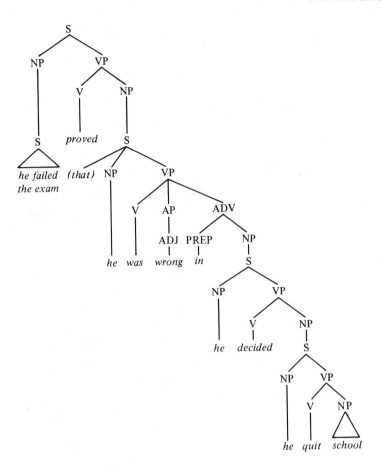

The rules required for converting this structure into the original sentence are more straightforward, but the structure is less informative about semantic interpretation:

He failed ⎫
↓   ↓ ⎬ the exam proved that he was wrong
His failing ⎭

in he decided he quit school.
         ↓   ↑
      deciding   to

Summary

For every respect in which the abstract tree-diagram he proposes is different from Surface Structure, a linguist must provide justification. The general lines of possible justifications were suggested earlier when we noted the ways in which surface and abstract structures may differ (ORDER, CODING, DELETION, TRACER INSERTION, CATEGORY SWITCHING, SUBSTITUTE FORMS). All such justifications are ultimately based on claims about the meaning of the sentences being analyzed, or the grammaticality of those or related examples. The arguments may, nevertheless, at times appear to be quite remote from either of these fundamental criteria. We will return to types of syntactic arguments in Chapter VII. At this juncture it is important only to understand that the technique of assigning abstract tree-diagrams to sentences is motivated by the light it throws on semantic interpretation. In Chapter VII we will show that it is also motivated by the generalizations which are then more easily statable about such syntactic processes as nominalization, gerundive formation, infinitivalization (i.e., *to*-insertion), and a variety of others.

Types of Syntactic Rules

In Chapter IV we saw a short set of phrase-structure rules, or constituent-structure rules, which serve to summarize abstract tree-diagrams. Such rules are said to **generate** these diagrams, i.e., the rules can be applied over and over in different combinations to enumerate an unlimited number of tree-diagrams of sentences.

The rules can, in principle, be applied mechanically (e.g., by a computer), requiring no intervention of human 'knowledge of the language' to make them come out right. In that sense, they are completely explicit in what they assert about the structure of sentences. They provide a device to characterize one aspect of what we know about sentences, namely their internal hierarchical organization.

Within the theory of grammar that has flourished vigorously since the late 1950's under the leadership of Noam Chomsky at the Massachusetts Institute of Technology—a theory that has completely revitalized the study of grammar all over the world, regardless of what aspects of that theory ultimately survive the criticism and alternatives of later scholarship—these phrase-structure rules are taken as the basic rules of sentence formation. It is assumed that the initial symbol S for 'sentence' can be taken as the starting point of a sequence of analytic rules—rules like those of Chapter IV—each of which in turn analyzes the sentence into finer and finer constituents down to the basic wordlike units. It is NOT assumed—indeed, it has been explicitly denied, repeatedly—that this procedure reflects in any way what speakers do when they actually use language. Obviously speakers do not start out with the notion S in mind, and then say to themselves:

(1) Well, let's divide S into two parts, NP and VP.

(2) Now, for NP, I think I'll talk about a noun which has an indefinite quantifier.

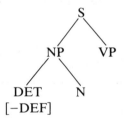

(3) Suppose the noun is *orchestra.*

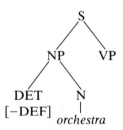

And so on. The procedure, viewed as something people might do, is too silly to pursue further. Whatever it is that speakers do, certainly they don't do this. Possibly they start at the other end, at the bottom of the tree, with words (or wordlike primitive semantic elements) that they combine, by some sort of synthesizing process, into larger units. More likely than either of these is that the process, while certainly a synthesizing one, deals with much more abstract units and groupings than those which we actually see and hear as words and sentences, and goes up and down, zigzagging, from more to less abstract and back, with interaction between elements at all levels.

Since we don't know much of anything substantial about how speakers store their extensive knowledge of their languages, or how they retrieve it and put it to use in forming sentences, we are free to build formal models which have NO NOTION OF MENTAL PROCESS WHATEVER built into them. They provide analogues to the CONTENT of what speakers know, but not analogues to the MENTAL STORAGE OR PROCESSING of that content. The various types of rules discussed below are to be understood in that sense.

Formation Rules

The formation rules of Chomskyan grammar, as indicated above, are phrase-structure rules like those given in Chapter IV for English. Such rules have the following properties:

1. Each rule applies directly to a single syntactic category symbol, whenever that symbol is the initial symbol of the derivation or has been generated by a previous rule. If there is a rule

   $$NP \rightarrow DET \quad N \quad (S)$$

   then any time there is an NP anywhere in the derivation, this rule must apply to give either

   ```
        NP
       /  \
      /    \
    DET    N
   ```

   or

   ```
          NP
        / | \
       /  |  \
     DET  N   S
   ```

2. Each rule applies regardless of the structure around the item to which it applies. Whether the NP of the example above is the subject-NP, as in

   ```
       S
      / \
     /   \
    NP   VP
   ```

or some NP far down the tree, as in

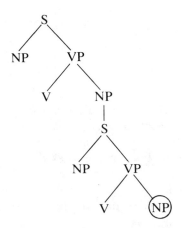

the same rule applies to assign internal structure to each NP.

3. No formation rule of this type is permitted to delete symbols. The following rule is, then, illegal under this condition, because it allows the NP to be deleted:

$$*NP \;\rightarrow\; \left\{ \begin{matrix} DET & N & (S) \\ & \emptyset & \end{matrix} \right\}$$

4. No formation rule of this type, or sequence of rules of this type, is permitted to permute symbols. The following rule is illegal under this condition, because it permutes NP and VP:

$$*NP \;\; VP \;\rightarrow\; VP \;\; NP$$

These conditions on phrase-structure formation rules are needed in order to guarantee that there will be a unique mapping relation between the rules and the trees that they are intended to characterize. The first condition guarantees that two symbols will not be merged into a single unit. It outlaws rules like these:

$$*V \;+\; NP \;\rightarrow\; VP$$

If 'merger' rules were not outlawed, we could not examine a string of categories and determine whether a rule had applied or not, since a merger rule effectively REVERSES an expansion rule:

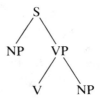

The second condition defines a particular type of phrase-structure rule, what is known as a **context-free** rule. At some point in a derivation, it is necessary to examine the context and make decisions which are SENSITIVE to that context. For our purposes that point can be postponed until the bottom of the derivation, where words are looked up and attached to the category symbols; we will then be employing **context-sensitive** rules. For example, if our tree has the shape

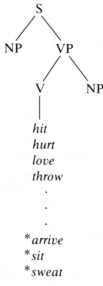

we will attach to V only a verb that can be followed by some NP (i.e., only a transitive verb):

The third condition, prohibiting deletions, is really another form of the first condition, since if nodes could be deleted, we could not know whether or not a rule had applied:

                          (NP)—delete by rule below

        *RULE: V + NP → V

The tree AFTER this rule has applied looks intransitive (no object), but it was initially generated by the rule that creates transitive VP's.

The fourth condition, prohibiting permutations, guarantees that the relation of category membership will not be violated. For example, if we had a rule like this:

    *NP VP → VP NP

then we could derive the following tree:

```
              S
            /   \
          NP     VP
          |      |
          VP     NP
```

But notice that this says that VP is an NP, and NP is a VP (the vertical lines), which we surely do not want to say, or else the whole point of syntactic categories goes down the drain.

Other Kinds of Formation Rules

Several types of rules can be used for matching tree-diagrams to linear strings (i.e., assigning constituent structure to sentences). It is possible, for example, to use bottom-up synthesis rules which result in trees that are identical to those generated by top-down analysis rules. So, for example, given the string:

ART   N   V   PREP   ART   N
The   boy left in   the   afternoon

and the rules

1. ART N   =   NP

2. PREP NP   =   PrepP

3. V PrepP   =   VP

4. NP VP   =   S

we can apply them to the string to construct this tree:

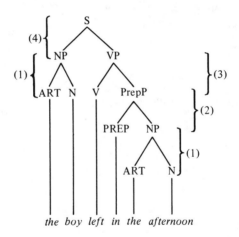

the boy left in the afternoon

We can, in the same way, start from words in the dictionary which are marked as to what syntactic classes they can combine with, and we can build up atomic sentences and complex clusters of them simply by observing the lexical restrictions on what can combine with what.

The details of different types of formation rules are unimportant; what is important is that formation rules can characterize ONLY ONE STRUC-TURE, WITH ONLY ONE MEANING, AT A TIME. But real sentences, we have noted repeatedly, are often ambiguous; and real sentences are often paraphrases of other sentences in systematic ways (recall in Chapter I the many versions of *Computers retrieve information easily*). Neither of these fundamental relations between linear strings and their meanings—ambiguity and synonymy/paraphrase—can be captured by formation rules alone. Some other kind of rule is needed.

Transformational Rules

Ambiguity is a one-to-many relation wherein a single Surface Structure has two or more meanings. To characterize this relation, we need rules which have the effect of merging two (or more) abstract structures—tree-diagrams which at least approximately characterize the different meanings—into a single Surface Structure. Such rules clearly must have a certain property which formation rules do not have; namely, they must operate on STRUCTURES, not just on single symbols—they must change one tree-diagram into another tree-diagram, since in no other way could they bring about mergers of distinct structures.

Synonymy/paraphrase, on the other hand, is a many-to-one relation wherein two or more Surface Structures have only a single meaning. To characterize this relation, we need rules which, starting from a single abstract Semantic Structure, have the effect of converting it into two or more distinct Surface Structures. Such rules would necessarily have exactly the same distinctive property that we've just seen is needed to deal with ambiguity: they must operate on structures, not just on single symbols.

A type of rule which has this property is called a **transformational** rule—one which operates ACROSS (Lat. *trans-*) FORMATIONS, i.e., one which changes formations into other formations, trees into other trees.

Formally, a transformational rule has two parts:

1. A **structure index** (SI) which characterizes the sentence pattern (the set of trees), the **input,** to which the rule is applicable.
2. A **structure change** (SC) which characterizes those respects in which the **output** of the rule differs from the input.

A structure index typically has two parts:

1. A string of category symbols (constants) intermixed with variables (X, Y, Z). The purpose of the variables is to make the structure index as general as possible. For instance, suppose we wish to specify a set of trees which start out

   NP V

   and can then be followed by anything without affecting the output of the rule, e.g.,

   NP V NP
   NP V ADV
   NP V NP   ADV
   NP V NP   NP   ADV

It would be impossible to characterize EVERYTHING that can follow the V by actually listing it; so instead we merely use X as a variable over all possible strings that can follow NP in this rule:

NP V X

This says that the rule applies to an NP immediately followed by V, and whatever follows the V is irrelevant.

2. A set of conditions under which the structure index is applicable. For instance, suppose a certain rule applies to the structure index

NP V NP

only if the first NP and the second NP refer TO THE SAME INDIVIDUAL, as in

John hates John.

where *John* refers to the same individual (as in *John hates himself*). We can specify this in a condition:

SI: NP V NP

      1   2   3

Condition: 1 = 3

The numbers merely make it easier to find our way around in the SI. It is easier to say '1 = 3' than 'The first NP refers to the same individual as the second NP.'

The format outlined above for structure indices is essentially standard among all transformational grammarians. The format for showing a structure change is not so well standardized, and in fact the one which is most widely used is somewhat difficult to read and not without challenge as to its adequacy. It works like this: assign numbers to the structure index (as above). Below these numbers write new numbers and constants in such a way as to reflect the changes you want the rule to effect. A simple example is this:

         He expects –   he   will leave
SI: NP   V $_S$[NP AUX V X]

       1   2   3   4   5

Condition: 1 = 3

SC: 1 2 Ø *to* 5

Now compare just the lines of numbers:

SI: 1   2   3   4   5

       ↓   ↓   ↓   ↓   ↓

SC: 1   2   Ø   *to*   5

Another way of saying the same thing is this:

SI: NP   V $_S$[NP   AUX   V X]

        1   2   3   4   5

SC: (1) Delete 3

       (2) Replace 4 with *to*

Whichever way it is stated, the EFFECT is the following:

He expects – he   will   leave

              ↓   ↓

              Ø   *to*

or, more generally,

NP   V $_S$[NP   AUX   V   X]

          ↓   ↓

          Ø   *to*

thereby covering not only this sentence but all others of the same form:

He expects (that) he will fail the exam tomorrow.
→   He expects to fail the exam tomorrow.

Mary hopes (that) she will have a ten-pound baby.
→   Mary hopes to have a ten-pound baby.

.
.
.

Transformations:
Types of Structure Change

Viewed superficially in terms of what the structure change does to its input (a tree that meets the structure index), transformations are of four types:

1. Deletion rules
2. Substitution rules
3. Insertion rules
4. Movement rules

    The four types are mnemonically named. Deletion rules delete some element from the input; substitution rules substitute an element for some other element; insertion rules insert an additional element; and movement rules switch the order of elements. Below are examples of each.

DELETION

John is taller than Mary is.

↓

∅

→   John is taller than Mary.

The girl who is talking with John is my sister.

↓ ↓

∅ ∅

→   The girl talking with John is my sister.

The idiot whom we elected will resign.

↓

∅

→   The idiot we elected will resign.

SUBSTITUTION

My car struck the pedestrian before I saw the pedestrian.

↓

him

→   My car struck the pedestrian before I saw *him.*

John plays the cello, and Mary plays the cello, too.

↓

does

→ John plays the cello, and Mary *does*, too.

In what way did he manage to do that?

↓

how

→ *How* did he manage to do that?

For what reason did he leave?

↓

why

→ *Why* did he leave?

INSERTION

Is a doctor in the room?

↑

there

→ Is *there* a doctor in the room?

John admitted   he was drunk.

↑

that

→ John admitted *that* he was drunk.

_ _ *John*   is failing, not *Mary*.

↑ ↑   ↑

it is   who

→ *It is John who* is failing, not *Mary*.

MOVEMENT

She put on her dress.

She put her dress on.

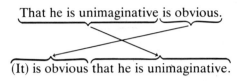

That he is unimaginative is obvious.

(It) is obvious that he is unimaginative.

The study of the formal properties of rules is an enormous separate topic involving, for example, technical questions about the relative capacity of different types; e.g., do we need, in order to account for the characteristics of natural languages, devices like transformational rules, which are virtually unlimited in their capacity to describe ANY two structures as being related even though we don't want them to be? We will not pursue these formal questions further here, but instead turn to a different way of looking at types of rules.

Transformations: Types of Domain

Among the differences that can be discerned in the domains (the structure indices) to which transformations apply, perhaps the most important is that between rules which operate only within a single sentence (i.e., only within a structure dominated by S, without crossing over into a structure dominated by another S either at the same level or above or below), and rules whose domain is not restricted this way. Among those rules which are not restricted to a single S, some are restricted to at most two S's, whereas others are unbounded with respect to the number of S's across which they operate. Let us consider first the most restricted type, those that cannot cross ANY higher or lower sentential (clause) boundary: we may call them **clause-internal** rules.

In **Dative-shift**, the 'receiver' or 'patient' (expressed here by *to his son*) can be moved from final position to the position immediately after the verb:

He left a fortune (to his son)

→   He left his son a fortune.
        ↑

> (*to* → Ø because serial order sufficiently marks the indirect object)

But it cannot be moved on up into the next higher clause:

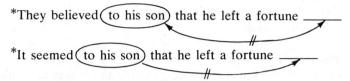

There is another rule, called **Complex-NP-shift**, which moves an NP to the end of its own clause if the NP is a complex one (e.g., contains a relative clause):

I disliked (the boys I used to go to school with) very much

→   I disliked very much the boys I used to go to school with.

This rule does not apply if the NP is a simple one:

I disliked my schoolmates very much.
↛   *I disliked very much my schoolmates.

But the rule can shift a heavy NP only to the end of its own clause; it cannot move it clear to the end of the whole sentence in which that clause is embedded:

The fact that I disliked very much

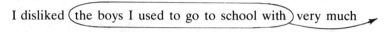

↛   *The fact that I disliked very much was obvious the boys I used to go to school with.

Another rule, called **Each-shift**, moves *each* to either of two alternative positions within its own clause:

(Each) of the golfers birdied four holes

→   The golfers each birdied four holes.
→   The golfers birdied four holes each.

But the rule cannot move the word *each* beyond the bounds of its own clause:

The fact – that each of the golfers birdied four holes – annoyed the spectators.

→   The fact – that the golfers birdied four holes each – annoyed the spectators.

↛   *The fact – that the golfers birdied four holes – annoyed the spectators each.

The **Passive** rule has the effect of exchanging the positions of the semantic agent and the semantic object, moving the object into subject position:

John expected Mary.
→   Mary was expected by John.

The sentence below has a clause as object of the higher verb *expect:*

John expected – Mary would arrive.

The object is the whole clause *Mary would arrive,* and not just the NP *Mary* that immediately follows the verb *expect.* It is impossible to move *Mary* up to be subject of *expect* by the Passive rule, because the Passive would then be applying across the boundary of the lower sentence:

*Mary was expected by John would arrive.
*Mary was expected would arrive by John.

The rule which has been proposed to create **reflexive** pronouns in the right places in English operates only within simplex sentences (i.e., is clause-internal). The indices (i, j) on NP's below are intended to indicate that they refer to the same individual:

John$_i$ shaved John$_i$.
→   John shaved himself.

But if the second *John$_i$* appears outside the simplex in which the first *John$_i$* appears, the reflexive pronoun is ungrammatical:

John$_i$ asked Mary$_j$ to shave John$_i$.
↛   *John asked Mary to shave himself.
      cf. John asked Mary to shave him.

John$_i$ asked Mary$_j$ if she$_j$ would shave John$_i$.
↛   *John asked Mary if she would shave himself.
      cf. John asked Mary if she would shave him.

There is a second type of rule which is limited to its own clause plus one more—i.e., it can move an element up into the next higher clause, or down into the next lower clause. Perhaps the best-studied rule of this type is **Raising**.[1] There are certain predicates which can take sentential subjects:

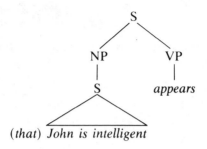

Some of these (like *appear*) are grammatical only in a form that results from moving the sentential subject out to the right of the predicate (by a rule called **Extraposition**, discussed below):

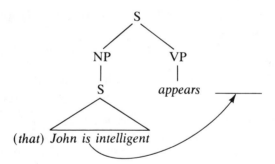

Others (like *certain*) are grammatical without Extraposition, but are much improved if Extraposition has operated:

> It appears (that) John is intelligent.
> It is certain (that) John will write a good book.
>   cf. That John will write a book is certain.

With sentences of this type, the rule of Raising can apply, lifting the subject of the sentence on the right up into the subject slot of the higher predicate:

---

[1] Postal (1974) is devoted entirely to the ramifications of this one rule.

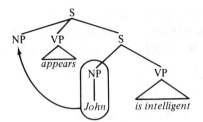

→   John appears to be intelligent.

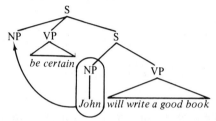

→   John is certain to write a good book.

Furthermore, the rule may apply twice (or more) if there is an appropriate higher predicate:

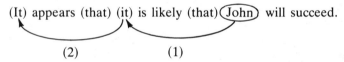

(2)   (1)

(1) It appears that John is likely to succeed.
(2) John appears (to be) likely to succeed.

The same rule applies to sentences where a verb from a certain subclass has a sentential object, with the important difference that the subject of the lower sentence is raised into the OBJECT slot in relation to the higher verb:

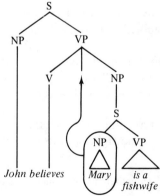

John believes ↖ ─(Mary) is a fishwife.

→   John believes Mary to be a fishwife.

If we use a pronoun (*she*/*her*) as subject of the lower sentence, it is clear that it must change to object form after it is raised:

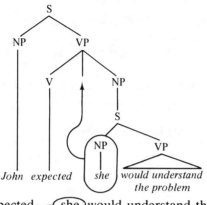

John expected ↖ ─(she) would understand the problem.

→   John expected her to understand the problem.

There is another type of Raising, unrelated to the type discussed above, in which the DIRECT OBJECT is raised out of the sentential subject clause with a certain class of predicates, and becomes the derived subject of the next higher predicate. This rule has been called by the curious name **Tough-movement** (based on the fact that *tough* is one of the possible higher predicates, as in *John is tough to please*/*It is tough to please John*).[2] Some examples:

(It) is difficult to account for (Mary)

→   Mary is difficult to account for.

(It) is impossible to justify (his behavior)

→   His behavior is impossible to justify.

(It) is a terrible thing to waste (a mind)

→   A mind is a terrible thing to waste.

[2] In the history of transformational grammar, several scholars have given humorous names like Pied Piping, Tough-movement, and Sluicing to syntactic rules. Unfortunately such names, a few years later, are neither mnemonic nor transparent in their meaning.

The three types of Raising discussed above involve only NP's. In the type below, the negative adverb is raised from a lower sentence into the next higher one:

I think she has not arrived yet.

→   I don't think she has arrived yet.

I suppose we ought not consider that alternative.

→   I don't suppose we ought to consider that alternative.

In **Modal-lowering**, a logically higher predicate of a certain type is lowered into the VP of the next sentence down:

It is possible (that) he fail the exam.

→   He $\begin{Bmatrix} \text{might} \\ \text{may} \end{Bmatrix}$ fail the exam.

Logically, the Modal-lowering operation might be represented this way in a more abstract diagram:

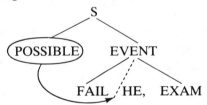

Negatives also probably can be considered to originate as higher predicates which get lowered into the VP:

It is not the case (that) he failed the exam.

→   He didn't fail the exam.

Logically, the operation is parallel to Modal-lowering:

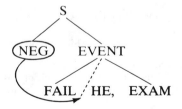

In Chapter II, we saw reasons for considering some types of adverbs as higher predicates. Since they appear on the surface to be modificational in structure, subordinated to some other category, there must be rules to lower them and change their category identification:

ADJ
He is frank in stating his views.

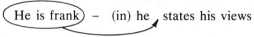

ADV
→   He frankly states his views.

ADV
→   He states his views frankly.

ADJ
The action of his writing books is frequent.

ADV
→   He frequently writes books.

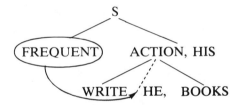

From the examples above, it is apparent that Raising is different from Lowering in an important respect. When Raising takes place, the structure of the lower sentence may be slightly modified to make the Surface Structure more transparent (e.g., the use of tracer elements like *to* in the Raising examples above). But when predicates are lowered (as in Modal-, NEG-, and Adverb-lowering—all of which are merely different labels for types of **Predicate-lowering**, with the labels assigned in accordance with the category to which they belong on the surface), the structure of the higher sentence is DESTROYED. The higher predicate is absorbed into the lower sentence and there is no trace, except semantically, of the original structure.

To see that Raising and Lowering rules apply to move elements into the NEXT higher or lower clause, consider this example:

It appears that it is certain that John will arrive on time.

Now, both *appears* and *certain* are predicates which permit Subject-raising. If the rule could apply from any lower sentence up into any higher sentence that has an appropriate predicate, we should get:

*John appears that it is certain to arrive on time.

But in fact we must FIRST raise the subject into the next higher sentence, and then it can be raised to the still higher sentence:

(1) It appears that John is certain to arrive on time.
(2) John appears to be certain to arrive on time.

STAGE (1):

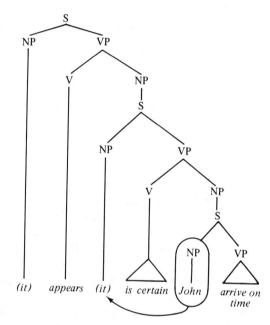

STAGE (2):

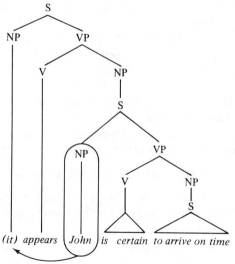

So far, then, we have seen clause-internal rules and two-clause rules (limited to movement into one above, or one below). The third type, on the basis of domain restrictions, is **unbounded**. Elements are moved by these rules from lower clauses into the highest clause. They are not restricted to the NEXT higher clause. Unboundedness is a property of rules which also share a particular semantic function; they are all **focusing**[3] rules (but not all focusing rules are unbounded; e.g., Passive is a clause-internal focusing rule). Typical examples are the following:

WH-FRONTING

⤴John wants *WH‑something.*

(WH- flags the item on which the interrogative is focused.)
→   What does John want?
⤶ John wants to consider the possibility of persuading Mary to buy
    WH₋something.

→   What does John want to consider the possibility of persuading
      Mary to buy?

CLEFTING

⤴John bought lots of *stock.*
→   It's *stock* that John bought lots of.
⤶ John wanted to explore the possibility of persuading his broker
    to buy stock in *IBM.*

→   It's *IBM* that John wanted to explore the possibility of
      persuading his broker to buy stock in.

Besides characterizing the domain of applicability in terms of one-clause, two-clause, and multiple-clause (unbounded) rules, we need to distinguish between rules that apply only to the topmost S, and those that apply within lower clauses. There is a rule, for example, which moves an auxiliary verb into the second position of a sentence which begins with an interrogative word; but the rule applies ONLY IF the sentence is not itself embedded. It is called **WH-AUX-attraction**:

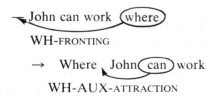

⤸John can work (where)

WH-FRONTING

→   Where John (can) work

WH-AUX-ATTRACTION

→   Where can John work?

---

[3] Discussed in Chapter VI.

But now suppose we embed the sentence as object of *know:*

I don't know 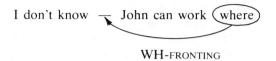 John can work where

WH-FRONTING

→   I don't know where John can work.

We cannot now apply WH-AUX-attraction, or we would get the ungrammatical string,

*I don't know where can John work.

NEG-fronting provides a similar situation:

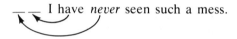 I have *never* seen such a mess.

→   Never have I seen such a mess.

I claim that I have never seen such a mess.

↛   ?*I claim that never have I seen such a mess.

Interaction of Rules

All the rules so far listed make up only a fraction of those needed for English. It is apparent that to describe the complex interactions between them would be a task well beyond the limits of this introductory text. (In fact, the total job is still well beyond the capabilities of current linguistic theory, although the task is much further advanced than we have attempted to show.) There are two principles which simplify the interaction of these numerous rules, (1) **rule government** and (2) **rule ordering**.

A rule is said to be governed when a particular word or class of words must be present in the sentence before the rule can apply. Raising, for example, is a governed rule; it can take place only if the next higher predicate belongs to the class of predicates that are lexically marked as accepting this rule:

likely
certain
appear
seem
expect   } Lexically marked for RAISING
believe
.
.
.

probable
possible
demand
deny   } RAISING disallowed
.
.
.

For example:

It is likely that John left.
→   John is likely to have left.
It seems that John has left.
→   John seems to have left.
John expected that Mary would have left.
→   John expected Mary to have left.

But not:

It is probable that John left.
↛   *John is probable to have left.
John demanded that Mary leave.
↛   *John demanded Mary to leave.

The best-established principle of rule ordering is that of **cyclic rule application**, one which we have been using implicitly all along. It simply requires that to derive a surface tree from an abstract one, the rules must be applied first to the lowest clause(s) in the tree, then to the next higher one(s), and so on up to the top:

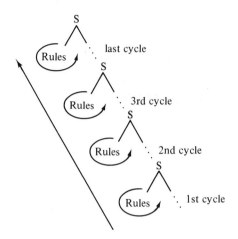

For example:

Mary is expected to persuade Pat to badger John into being examined by the doctor.[4] (See diagram on p. 139.)

On the S_3 cycle, Passive is applied:

the doctor examine John
→   John be examined by the doctor

On the S_2 cycle, **Gerundivization**, triggered by the PREP *into*, applies
downward into S_3:

... into John be examined by the doctor
→   ... into John's being examined by the doctor

Also on the S_2 cycle, **Equi-NP-deletion**, triggered by the identity of *John*
in S_2 with *John* in S_3, applies to delete the lower occurrence:

... John into John's being examined by the doctor
→   ... John into being examined by the doctor

On the S_1 cycle, Equi-NP-deletion, this time triggered by the identity of
Pat in S_1 with *Pat* in S_2, applies to delete the lower occurrence; this leaves

---

[4] Several of the rules mentioned below have not been exemplified yet, but they will
be, shortly.

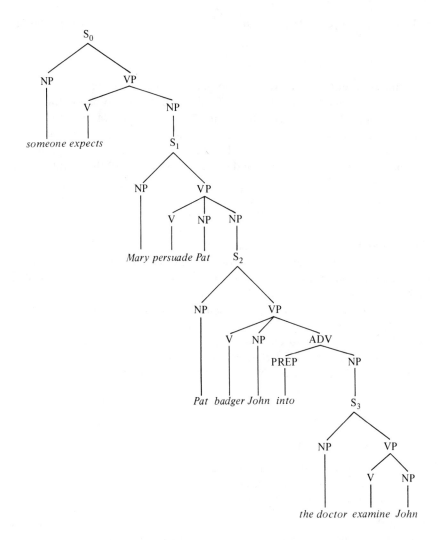

a finite verb *badger* without a subject, so that **Infinitive-marking** applies:

> . . . Pat to badger John into being examined by the doctor

On the S_0 cycle, *Mary* is raised to become direct object of *expect*, thereby once again leaving a finite verb, *persuade*, without a subject, so that Infinitive-marking applies once again:

> . . . Mary to persuade Pat to badger John into being examined by the doctor

Still on the S_0 cycle, Passive can apply to *someone expects Mary*, giving:

Mary is expected by someone to persuade Pat to badger John into being examined by the doctor.

And finally, **Indefinite-agent-deletion** gets rid of *by someone*.

Thus the order of application of rules is determined by (1) the cycle and (2) applicability as defined by the structure index of the rule itself (which also specifies whether it is governed or not). Some versions of grammatical theory also require that (3) rules be extrinsically ordered (i.e., assigned numbers and applied strictly in accord with those numbers).

Derived Structure

Recall that a transformational rule applies to a given structure, and from it derives a new structure. Wherever possible, the structure of the source is retained in the output. But transformational rules do some things which make it impossible to retain all parts of the source structure. We may need (1) to eliminate unwanted structure after lower nodes have been deleted, or (2) to build in additional structure after something has been moved. The necessity to eliminate unwanted structure, or **Tree-pruning**, is evident when embedded clauses are substantially reduced. Do we still want to have the node S on top of the truncated remainder? For example:

SEMANTIC REPRESENTATION

APPEAR (INTELLIGENT, JOHN)

SURFACE PARAPHRASES

It appears that John is intelligent.
John appears to be intelligent.
John appears intelligent.

Taking these three surface forms as semantically equivalent, we note that the first obviously contains a subordinate sentence (noun clause):

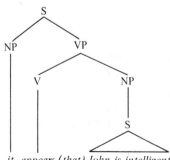

it   appears (that) John is intelligent

The second results from raising *John* up to the subject of the higher verb *appears:*

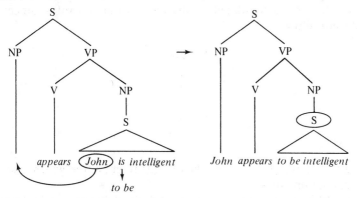

Now, the S-node circled in the right-hand phrase-marker above is the one in question. *To be intelligent* has lost most of the properties of sentence-hood; it is ABSTRACTLY a sentence, but once it has been truncated in this way, is it still proper to have the node S above it? In the third paraphrase, one is even more likely to feel that the S should be eliminated from the tree, and also the NP above the S:

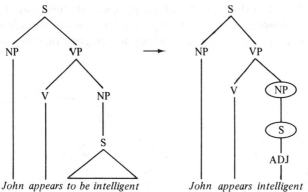

Some general procedure must be established to prune out the unwanted nodes, since the surface tree should look like this:

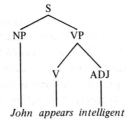

One way to do this (though some unsolved problems remain) is to require that the output of the rule be inspected to determine whether it conforms to the POSSIBLE trees stipulated by the basic formation rules. Since those rules do not allow

we can delete both of the nodes above ADJ to get a tree which IS allowed by the formation rules.

The other aspect of the problem of derived structure is building new structure. Consider an example:

The enemy destroyed the city.
The enemy's destruction of the city (. . . was total).

If we assume that *enemy's destruction* is derived from *enemy destroyed* by a nominalization transformation, which in spite of numerous technical difficulties is a reasonable assumption on the basis of our intuitions about the semantics, then some complex shifting in category membership must be explained:

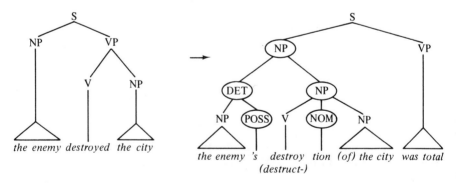

Somehow all the circled nodes must be supplied, since they are not present in the input tree. They can perhaps be supplied by the procedure suggested above: derive a string by the transformational rule, and then subject it to reanalysis through the formation rules. It is not clear, however, that this very complex procedure is the best approach to this problem. There are, in fact, so many difficulties inherent in this proposal that some linguists have argued that the relation between the two trees above is not transformational at all, that the two must be independently derived by the formation rules, and that the obvious relations between them would be captured by features in the lexicon (e.g., *destroy* and *destruction* would have similar semantic characterizations). We leave the matter open, for the introductory purposes of this book.

Summary

We have now considered some of the superficial formal aspects of formation rules and transformational rules: what they look like, what sorts of things they can and can't do, what their domains of application are, how they interact, how they assign Surface Structure after they have applied to more abstract structures. We now turn to their COMMUNICATIVE functions, to relate these abstract and rather esoteric linguistic constructs to the aims and needs of people talking with one another.

Communicative Functions
of Syntactic Rules

Language has **pragmatic functions**. We can perhaps get a clearer idea about the needs that are served by the variety of syntactic devices found in languages if we examine broadly a typical human transaction in which language is used. We may think of the minimum number of participants as two, a speaker and a hearer. The total transaction can be called a **discourse**. Within the discourse, sentences can be used for various purposes: e.g., to make assertions, to give commands, to provide reassurance, to make promises, to request information, to persuade, to introduce new information, to deceive, and so on through the entire gamut of objectives that speech acts might have. Corresponding to some of these aims, most languages have special syntactic forms like **declarative** sentences (the form for making assertions), **presentative** sentences (for introducing new information), **interrogative** sentences (for asking questions and making requests), and **imperative** sentences (for giving commands). For others of the aims, language may not provide special forms. Rather, it may be necessary to include within the sentence a lexical specification of the aim; e.g., to get the hearer to understand a certain sentence as a promise, the speaker may have to say, *I promise that*.... On the other hand, in the right context, the simple statement *I will* can be understood only as a promise.

From this it should be clear that the transaction between speaker and hearer must include, for most sentences, two kinds of meaning:

1. The **substance**: what is predicated about what or whom. This is called the **propositional content** by logicians, and it has two aspects that are now familiar to the reader from earlier chapters; a **predicational** aspect, and a **referring** aspect, corresponding approximately to verbs and noun phrases respectively.
2. The **intention**: what is the relation of the substance to the speaker, to the hearer, to the rest of the world? That is, by uttering the substance, does the speaker intend to inform the hearer, question him, command him, warn him, apologize to him, welcome him, or what? Some kinds of intent may be represented logically by a higher predicate, selected from the class of **performative** verbs, with *I* as subject and *you* as indirect object:

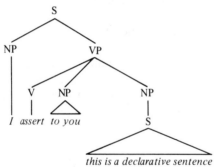

→   (I assert to you that) This is a declarative sentence.

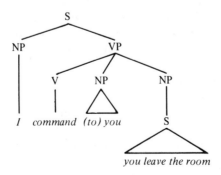

→   (I command you that you should) Leave the room.

The parenthesized material—the PERFORMATIVE structure which states the intent of the speech act—is deleted in simple declaratives, questions, and commands in English (and most languages), but other performatives are usually retained: *I promise you...*, *I beg you...*, *I urge you...*, etc.

Now, with regard to both substance and intention, the speaker can hardly get started at all unless he knows the answer to a wide range of questions about himself, the hearer, and the world. For instance, consider just the referring aspect of communicating substance. If the speaker wants to refer to a certain individual, he must know, or determine, whether that individual is already known to the hearer or not. If he assumes that the individual is unknown to the hearer, he might initiate the discourse with a PRESENTATIVE structure:

There's a guy who works in my office, named Swami.

Or he might initiate it with a question:

Do you know that guy named Swami who works in my office?

If he knows that Swami is an acquaintance of the hearer's, he can refer to him by name immediately: but a question of INTENTION may affect the form of the reference. Suppose he wants to warn the hearer about some aspect of Swami's behavior that the speaker assumes will come as an unpleasant surprise to the hearer:

That S.O.B. Swami has been spreading stories about you.

But in order for the speaker to bring up this kind of information with the hearer at all, it must be the case that he has a certain social relation with the hearer; roughly, they are peers and they are on familiar terms.

As the discourse goes on—or as we examine any discourse that has ever occurred—it will become clear that with every sentence there are **presuppositions** which determine in part both the substantive and the intentional meaning, and which therefore play a direct role in the determination of the form chosen by the speaker for the expression of his substance and intent. A goal of the speaker is to deepen the pool of information and presuppositions that he shares with the hearer, thereby reducing the burden of communication by eliminating the need to supply context.

There appear to be four main areas within which presuppositions must be shared (either in advance, or established in the course of the transaction) in order to grease the axles of communication:

1. There must be agreement on the kind of world within which the substance is to be taken as valid (i.e., the present real world, some imaginary world, some expected future world, some past world . . .)
2. There must be mutual accord concerning the speaker's knowledge and motivation, relative to the topic of the transaction.
3. The speaker must make some assumptions about the hearer's knowledge and interests, relative to the topic.
4. There must be certain assumptions about the social, cultural, geographical, and personal relations between the participants, which will determine the initial manner of approach and which will be constantly readjusted as the discourse proceeds.

Within the discourse, the speaker adopts certain **strategies** whose purpose is to ascertain what can safely be presupposed and to supply whatever cannot be. A strategy that appears to be characteristic of successful discourse over a wide range of natural languages is **incrementation**, which has two tactics:

1. Identifying explicitly that part of every sentence which represents old information—that which is context, that which provides continuity, that which links old with new, familiar with unfamiliar.
2. Adding new information in relatively small chunks, and, as long as it remains unchallenged, building on it as though it were fully shared OLD information.

From the preceding discussion we can infer that language, if it is an optimal system for satisfying these needs, is likely to provide devices for **foregrounding** new information and for **backgrounding** old information; devices for minimizing the repetition of referring expressions once the reference has been established; devices for maintaining continuity of topic; devices for calling explicit attention to change of topic; devices for introducing previously unshared referring expressions into the discourse; devices for attaching prominence to whatever the speaker views as most important—the substantive content, in some cases, the intent in others. These, then, are the pragmatic responsibilities of the language.

Tracer Functions

Language must handle these pragmatic assignments in a linear format, a sequence of words occurring through time, that also provides explicit evidence to enable the hearer to deduce correctly the hierarchical relationships that are part of the meaning. We have seen a number of instances where the Surface Structure differed substantially from the abstract Logical Form of the sentence. Consider one more, this one having appeared as the climactic sentence of a television advertisement intended to induce the 'have's' to loosen their purse strings on behalf of the education of the 'have-not's'. To get the full force of it, one should read it slowly and pontifically:

A mind is a terrible thing to waste.

It appears to say that 'a mind is a terrible thing—in some particular respect'. But of course we do not understand it that way at all. In fact, we do not understand it as saying ANYTHING directly about a mind. Rather, we understand it as equivalent to

To waste a mind is a terrible thing for someone to do.

This, in turn, is equivalent to

The action of wasting a mind is a terrible action.

This can be still further specified, to clarify the meaning of *is terrible:*

The action of wasting a mind is to be classified among those actions of which we disapprove strongly.

In its Logical Form (leaving out the performative *I assert to you*), the sentence is (roughly) this:

TERRIBLE (ACTION (WASTE (X, MIND)))

where X is the individual responsible for wasting a mind. In a tree-diagram:

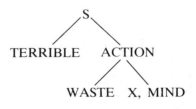

But if we analyze the sentence directly in its surface form, we have:

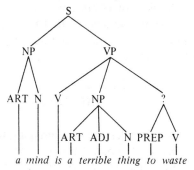

Between the Logical Form and the Surface Structure we note numerous differences:

1. More syntactic classes on the surface (the Logical Form has only the equivalent of nouns and verbs).
2. Only one 'clause' structure on the surface, as compared with two abstract ones (*Action is terrible* and *Someone waste a mind*).
3. *A mind* is subject of the surface sentence. In the Logical Form, it shows up as object of the embedded verb *waste*.
4. Several words in the surface sentence have no direct equivalent in the Logical Form: *a*, *is*, *thing*, and *to*.

Some of the differences above can be attributed to pragmatic considerations; e.g., *mind* is taken as subject of the surface sentence because it is directly linked to the preceding context of the discourse. Once this decision has been made (to raise *mind* from object of the lower predicate up to subject of the higher predicate), then various things have to be done to guarantee that its REAL relationship to the rest of the sentence can be recovered. In particular, the word *to* is inserted to mark the subordinate relation between *terrible* (the higher verb) and *waste* (the lower one). It is a tracer element. Likewise, the surface verb *is* has no function except to mark *terrible* as being the main predicate. Finally, the word *thing* is inserted into the sentence,

A mind is terrible to waste.

because without *thing*, the sentence does not instantly suggest that the mind is BEING wasted; it can be understood, instead, as parallel to

A bike is dangerous to ride.

which has one reading that includes *dangerous bike*, whereas our sentence does not include *terrible mind*.

Given, then, the initially pragmatic decision to raise *mind* into the leftmost position in the sentence—to **topicalize** it—there are other changes that serve to provide tracers for RECOVERY OF THE LOGICAL FORM. So far, then, our examination of communicative needs has shown two reasons for the variety of syntactic devices that may appear, superficially, only to mutilate the underlying logical structure: PRAGMATIC CONSIDERATIONS and LOGICAL RECOVERY.

Efficiency

Another reason that syntactic rules are so damaging to Logical Forms is for efficiency, in two senses: (1) compactness or brevity and (2) ease of processing. Let us suppose that some system of logical notation exists which is absolutely precise in the sense that the cognitive content, the truth value, of any message whatever can be represented consistently and unambiguously, with well-defined truth conditions for every proposition that can be asserted. It could then be said to meet with complete adequacy a criterion of RELIABILITY. From what is known of logic, however, one can deduce that the form of the message would not be COMPACT or BRIEF. Syntactic rules have, as one of their functions, the task of ABBREVIATING the form of the message, of making it more compact without losing its substance.

Consider this example where the Logical Form and Surface Structure are widely disparate, and where the virtue of brevity is more apparent than in previous examples:

John works more than Mary.
John works more than Mary does.
John works more than Mary works.

A tree-diagram of the third example looks like this:

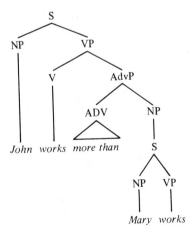

A first approximation of the abstract structure might be this:

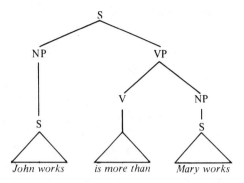

This presents some minor problems, like what sort of magic rule will change the predicate *is more than* into a mere adverb; but the most serious problem is that semantically this structure ENTAILS NOT ONLY THAT JOHN WORKS BUT ALSO THAT MARY DOES. The Surface Structure, however, does NOT entail that Mary works at all. It entails only that whatever may be the extent of working engaged in by Mary (including none at all), that extent is exceeded by the amount of work that John does: roughly,

> The extent to which John works exceeds the extent to which Mary works.

In an abstract phrase-marker, this structure would be:

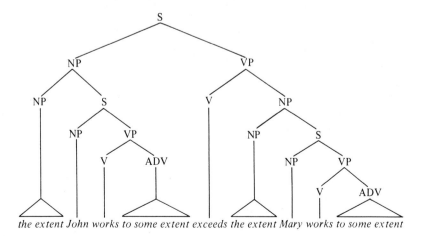

the extent John works to some extent exceeds the extent Mary works to some extent

The corresponding Logical Form, omitting many details, is this:

EXCEEDS {(EXTENT) (WORKING (JOHN'S))} {(EXTENT) (WORKING (MARY'S))}

or

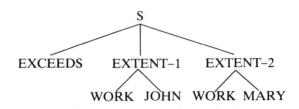

This can be made much more abstract and general,[1] including specification of the nature of the extent that is being measured (extent of duration, extent of intensity). But now we have gotten quite far away from the sentence *John works more than Mary.* What is obvious, now, is that the Surface Structure is very much more compact, very much briefer, than any version of the Logical Form that characterizes its meaning.

It is bewildering to contemplate the complexity of rules which would derive the comparative sentence from its Logical Form (or any similar or more general one). We can speculate on the types of rules that would be required:

1. LEXICALIZATION. The words written with capital letters in the Logical Form are not words but semantic chunks. The physical shape they manifest will vary unpredictably from language to language. Some sets of rules must explain, for example, when EXCEED is realized as *exceed* and when it is realized as *more than.*
2. SERIALIZATION. The Logical Form, written on paper, appears to have a serial order from left to right, but this is a consequence of presenting it in two-dimensional space. It is a purely hierarchical set of relations that could be represented on paper in any conventionalized order. There must therefore be rules which determine that a given hierarchical relationship will be serialized in a language as A–B or B–A. We discussed in Chapter III many of the considerations that enable languages to match up serially presented elements to particular hierarchical relations.
3. RAISING. There is no satisfactory way of representing the Logical Form of this sentence which would not have *John* and *Mary* at the bottom of the hierarchy. The predication EXCEEDS operates over two

---

[1] Bartsch and Vennemann (1972) provide a detailed analysis of the logical structures that underlie comparative sentences.

measure functions: (1) the extent of John's working and (2) the extent of Mary's working. Yet in the surface sentence, *John* and *Mary* are raised up into the highest nodes; *John* is subject, and he is compared directly with *Mary*. This is a reasonable pragmatic thing for syntax to do, since *John* and *Mary* are the foci of the conversation.

4. LOWERING. The top predicate in the Logical Form is EXCEEDS. In the surface sentence, it is lowered to adverbial form (lexicalized as *more than*). Since not all predicates can be lowered, somehow the rules must provide for lowering just the right ones (along with the correct lexicalization).

5. DELETION AND SUBSTITUTION. In our surface sentence, the entire predicate with *Mary* can be retained, or it can be deleted, or it can be replaced by the general action-verb substitute *does*. The syntax must explain why in this instance all three possibilities are grammatical whereas in other instances, apparently quite similar, the second predicate cannot be retained in its entirety:

> John devises better solutions than Mary.
> John devises better solutions than Mary does.
> John devises better solutions than Mary devises.
> *John devises better solutions than Mary devises solutions.

> John is more knowledgeable than Mary.
> John is more knowledgeable than Mary is.
> *John is more knowledgeable than Mary is knowledgeable.

> John smokes cigarettes more than Mary.
> John smokes cigarettes more than Mary does.
> *John smokes cigarettes more than Mary smokes.
> *John smokes cigarettes more than Mary smokes cigarettes.

In the face of such complexities as these that we would have to deal with if the syntactic rules were required LITERALLY to change an underlying Logical Form into a fully specified surface string, we will impose a less difficult task on the syntactic rules that we exemplify. It will be sufficient justification for the present purpose if it is true that such rules are necessary to link some reasonable abstract representation of a sentence to some near-surface representation. We reserve to Chapter VII the question of justifying particular rules.

Ease of Processing

The first aspect of efficiency, then, is brevity. The other aspect is that the recovery of the underlying structure must be possible in a way that conforms to processes which are comfortable for the immediate memory span of the human mind; i.e., language must structure the message in a way that makes it easy to decode. This task can be understood better by comparing these sentences:

(1a)   That she believes that he is correct proves that she loves him.
(1b)   Her belief in his correctness proves her love for him.

(2a)   The cheese that the rat that the cat chased ate was homogenized.
(2b)   The cheese that was eaten by the rat that was chased by the cat was homogenized.
(2c)   The cheese was homogenized that was eaten by the rat that was chased by the cat.

In (1a) above, it is apparent that processing is made difficult by having, as subject of *proves*, a sentence that contains another sentence within it; and by having several *he's* and *she's* to sort out. The nominalized version (1b) is much easier to process, in this instance. In (2a) above, we see that 'self-embedded' sentences are hard to figure out:

The cheese . . . . was homogenized.

   ↑

       that the rat . . . . ate

           ↑

          that the cat chased

By using the Passive form (2b–2c), we **close** each embedded sentence before we have to go on to process the next stretch, and having closed it, we can devote full attention to the remainder:

The cheese . . . . was homogenized.

   ↑

       that was eaten by the rat (CLOSE)

           ↑

          that was chased by the cat (CLOSE)

By postponing the relative clause that is attached to *cheese.* we can close all the syntactic linkages except the link back to the head:

The cheese was homogenized that was eaten by the rat that was chased
                                                                    by the cat.

OPEN LINK

Some types of syntactic rules seem to have this ease-of-processing function as their primary justification. In particular, all rules which shift material to the right within the same clause or within the next higher clause appear to be of this type. The best-known such rules are **Complex-NP-shift** and **Extraposition**. In Complex-NP-shift, any NP in the predicate which is somehow 'heavy', at least relative to what follows it, can be moved to the end of that clause:

He gave some money to his wife.

SIMPLE NP

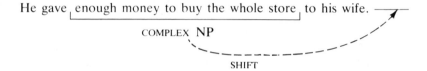

He gave enough money to buy the whole store to his wife.

COMPLEX NP

SHIFT

→   He gave to his wife enough money to buy the whole store.

Extraposition applies, most consistently, to move to the right those clauses which are subjects of predicates like *possible, obvious, necessary, important, desirable,* etc.:

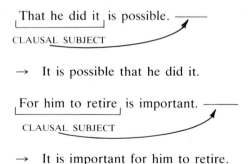

That he did it is possible.

CLAUSAL SUBJECT

→   It is possible that he did it.

For him to retire is important.

CLAUSAL SUBJECT

→   It is important for him to retire.

In general, however, this **stylistic** aspect of syntactic rules cannot be characterized simply in terms of whether a certain rule has or has not applied. The stylistic consequences of rule application depend on extremely complex interactions of syntax and lexicon. The use of nominalizations in the examples above (*her belief, his correctness, her love*) does indeed effectively simplify the processing, but in numerous other examples, the same device would obscure the meaning. Sentences like this one, loaded with nominalizations, are rightly criticized by rhetoricians:

> Her attempt at persuasion of them in respect to the incorrectness of their analysis of the problem was a failure.
> i.e., She tried but failed to persuade them that they had analyzed the problem incorrectly.

Functional Differences among Syntactic Rules

We have now seen that there are three principal types of motivation for those radical mutilations of logical structures brought about by the syntactic rules that relate such structures to surface sentences:

1. PRAGMATIC motivations: foregrounding new information, maintaining continuity, introducing new referring expressions, checking on shared information, and the like.
2. LOGICAL motivations: providing tracers between a linearly structured surface sentence and a hierarchically structured meaning.
3. EFFICIENCY motivations: for brevity, and for ease of processing.

The lines between these rough categories are not always clear. Whether substitute words, like pronouns, serve the goal of efficiency (they certainly help), or whether they are mainly a pragmatic device for tagging previously mentioned and thereby established referents, is not an important issue. They obviously serve both functions. For most rules it is possible to make a reasonably well-motivated assignment to one of these three categories for the purpose of getting a clearer idea about the way syntactic rules are used in communicative strategies.

Hierarchical Focusing Rules

We may refer to the substance and intention of a sentence as its **message**. The form in which the message is represented is its **code**. 'Code' refers to

Surface Structure; 'message' refers to abstract logical structure. When we speak of focusing, we do not refer to any change in the substance of the message, only to changes in the way the message is coded relative to what preceded, to what is presupposed, and to what is most important in the speaker's intention. Focusing rules introduce special marking into the Surface Structure to set off some element or elements as new or important; they assign PROMINENCE to that part of the message which the speaker wants to place in the foreground, and they destress (place in the background) that part of the message which merely provides continuity with what preceded or which confirms the presuppositions that are shared.

Clearly, like other information that the speaker provides about his message, focusing can be coded in a variety of ways, e.g., by intonation, by morphology, by serial word order. To claim that some messages are coded in a specially focused way—in a **marked** way—it is necessary to have a normal construction in mind as the **unmarked** coding for that message. This will vary from language to language. In English, and generally in verb-medial languages, the unmarked position for a topic is first in the sentence, i.e., to the left in the written sentence. The unmarked position for the comment is to the right. This correlates with the common intonation pattern that has maximum prominence on the last noun or verb. The speaker raises his voice, as it were, where he wants the hearer to focus his attention:

$$\text{John likes music a } {}^{l}\text{o}_{t}.$$

This indicates that we both (speaker and hearer) know who John is, and we both know that he likes music; the speaker's comment is that John's liking of music is extensive. Put another way, the statement above is not an answer to *What does John like?* but rather to *How much does John like music?* The focus is on *how much.*

On the other hand, suppose the focus is on *music:*

$$\text{John likes } {}^{m}\text{u}_{s_i}{}_{c} \text{ a lot.}$$

The change in focus CAN be coded with intonation alone, as above. Or it can be coded by a specially marked construction, either the **Cleft** construction or the **Pseudo-cleft**:

CLEFT

$$\text{It's } {}^{m}\text{u}_{s_i}{}_{c} \text{ that John likes a lot.}$$

PSEUDO-CLEFT

What John likes a lot is $^mu_{s_{i_c}}$.

In both constructions, the coding includes intonation as well as special structure. There are important differences between the two, of course; they appear together here because they both are obvious focusing constructions. They share the name 'Cleft' because both take a unified predicate (... *likes music*) and strip it into two parts. They differ in several ways. The Pseudo-cleft can strip an action predicate into its 'predicateness' (represented by *do*) and its substantive meaning:

John plays the cello.
→   What John does is play the cello.

It cannot do this with a nonaction ('stative') predicate:

John likes music.
↛   *What John does is like music.

On the other hand, the Cleft cannot strip apart the inside of a predicate at all (not in standard American English, anyway, although there are dialects in which this is possible):

John plays the cello.
↛   *It's play the cello that John does.

The Pseudo-cleft is a focusing rule which places the predicate or some part of the predicate in an especially prominent position. The Cleft, on the other hand, can also assign prominence to the subject:

John is always claiming to be right.
→   It's John who's always claiming to be right.

Another construction in which part of the predicate is fronted for prominence is **Object-fronting** (sometimes called 'Y-movement'):

My quartet can play early Mozart.
→   Early Mozart my quartet can play.

This construction topicalizes the object IN CONTRAST WITH some other object that the speaker has in mind:

Early Mozart my quartet can play. But you should hear how we massacre Beethoven.

That is, Object-fronting is not merely a matter of placing the object leftmost in the sentence for prominence. Rather, its placement there makes it especially clear that the object is one of two or more alternatives that the speaker is stipulating (in the preceding or following contexts).

A quite different sort of Object-fronting is seen in the Passive construction, which permits the speaker to move the object into the normal topic position of the subject—leftmost in the sentence (thereby linking it directly to previous context)—and to focus on the comment that is being made about it:

FULL PASSIVE

> Someone composed that sonata in the eighteenth century.
> → That sonata was composed by someone in the eighteenth century.

AGENTLESS PASSIVE

> That sonata was composed in the eighteenth century.

Related to Object-fronting, at least in its stylistic effect of fore-grounding some part of the sentence by dislocating it from its 'normal' position, is **Adverb-fronting**:

ADVERB-FRONTING

> I must get down to serious work tomorrow.
> → Tomorrow I must get down to serious work.

> You'll find some nice cymbidiums out back.
> → Out back you'll find some nice cymbidiums.

Of the various fronting rules, the one that most obviously serves the function of focusing the attention of the hearer on new information (more precisely, on the DESIRE FOR information) is the interrogative WH-fronting rule:

WH-FRONTING

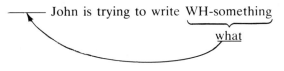

> → What is John trying to write?

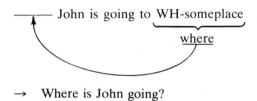

→   Where is John going?

In all 'information' questions like the ones above (including *what, where, when, why, how, which*), the WH-word must be moved to the front of the clause that is dominated, in its semantic representation, by the verb which specifies the intention of the sentence (the performative verb):

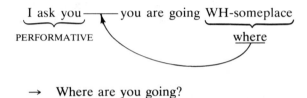

→   Where are you going?

This is also true even if the performative is not deleted; then the question clause is called an indirect question:

I asked him where he was going.

The auxiliary verb is attracted to the fronted WH-word only if the performative is deleted:

(I ask you) where you are going.
→   Where are you going?
       *Where you are going?
       *I ask you where are you going.

With respect to the function of focusing, a particularly interesting example is the **Presentative** construction that begins with *there* in English. What it does is introduce as a COMMENT some individual or class of individuals that the speaker intends to use as the topic of subsequent discourse. What the speaker wants to say, below, is that a certain restaurant exists with which the hearer is unfamiliar, and that they should get acquainted with it. He can't say,

We ought to try a restaurant down the street.

unless he means 'any old restaurant that happens to be down the street'.

He can say,

> We ought to try that restaurant down the street.

only if he has reason to believe the hearer is familiar with it. For what he wants to say, the presentative construction is designed:

> There's a restaurant down the street that we ought to try.

Important though the rules which produce such focusing structures as Clefts, Pseudo-clefts, Passives, Object-frontings, Adverb-frontings, and Presentatives are, they are relatively insignificant in the extent to which they mutilate semantic structure for pragmatic surface purposes. The most important focusing rules in this respect are the **Participant-raising** rules and the **Predicate-lowering** rules. We have seen these repeatedly throughout this and earlier chapters. Here we need only summarize some of the communicative motivations of such rules.

Typically the core message appears at the bottom of a semantic representation. We have seen many examples:

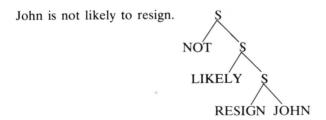

In such examples, and over an unlimited range of similar examples, the subject of the lowest predicate in the tree is raised up and coded as the HIGHEST subject. At the same time, modality and negative elements like POSSIBLE and NOT are lowered into the status of auxiliary verbs or adverbs.

The gains in Lowering and Raising rules are complementary to each other; less important predicates are subordinated, more important referring expressions and the most substantive predicate are given prominence. The Raising rules allow the subject slot of the surface sentence to be filled by a topic from some logically subordinate sentence. The Predicate-lowering rules, conversely, allow predicates whose logical domain is the whole surface sentence, or some large chunk of it, to be downgraded into secondary status while the substantive message is highlighted.

Coordinate Focusing Rules

In all the focusing structures discussed so far, the focusing rules bring about some READJUSTMENT within a logical hierarchy. There is a hierarchy before the rule applies, a different hierarchy afterward. In the rules discussed below, there is either (1) an assignment of hierarchical Surface Structure to a logically coordinate pair, or (2) the reverse of this, namely the elimination of logical subordination in favor of paratactic (coordinate) structure.

In the first category we have **relative clauses**. Under one proposal (though not the only one) about their logical structure, they are claimed to be coordinate predicates which share a referring expression (i.e., some NP):

The boy ⟋went to the hospital (and the boy broke his arm)

→   The boy *who broke his arm* went to the hospital.

By this rule, one of the conjoined clauses is forced into the background relative to the other, which thereby becomes the main assertion. The subordinate clause is the relative clause. It provides the background information necessary to IDENTIFY the boy, to put him into focus, if the speaker assumes the hearer is not acquainted with him. In case the speaker assumes that the hearer IS acquainted with the boy, he is likely to use the relative clause in a NONRESTRICTIVE or APPOSITIVE manner. It is then set off by a separate intonation contour (suggested by commas in English orthography) and merely provides additional background, but nonidentifying, information:

The boy ⟋went to the hospital (and the boy is my friend)

→   The boy, *who is my friend*, went to the hospital.

The identifying or restrictive type of relative clause occurs only with noun phrases. It can be substantially compressed under certain conditions:

The men (who)(are) working on the new sewer system deserve a raise in
pay.   ↓   ↓
              ∅   ∅

→   The men working on the new sewer system deserve a raise in pay.

The book (which)(is) on the table is by Tolstoy.
              ↓   ↓
              ∅   ∅

→   The book on the table is by Tolstoy.

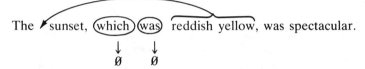

The ⚹ sunset, (which)(was) reddish yellow, was spectacular.
              ↓   ↓
              ∅   ∅

→   The reddish yellow sunset was spectacular.

The appositive type, on the other hand, may provide afterthought information or background for verb phrases or entire assertions:

They sent her to dancing school, and that $\begin{Bmatrix} \text{action} \\ \text{fact} \end{Bmatrix}$ annoyed me.

→   They sent her to dancing school, which annoyed me.

They set out to get married, and they *did* get married.

→   They set out to get married, which they *did.*

Relative clauses are one of the most extensively studied and best understood of the syntactic structures found in natural languages.

In the other category of coordinate focusing rules, in which logical subordination is lost in favor of paratactic structure, we find examples like the following:

John is leaving around noon, I think.

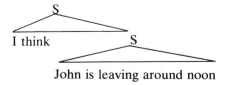

She's pretty, don't you think?

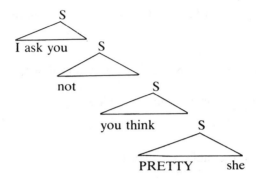

In such examples, one of the higher predicates is extracted and made into a paratactic 'tag' at the end of a sentence that then LOOKS LIKE the highest predication but turns out, when you reach the tag, to have been logically subordinate.

Compression Rules

Under this heading we have a range of syntactic devices that serve primarily to make sentences shorter. In **Conjunction-reduction**, elements that are identical in parallel structures are deleted:

John works late, (and Mary) works late.
$$\downarrow$$
$$\emptyset$$

→   John and Mary work late.

John could not find a viable solution, and John could not find an answer.
$$\downarrow$$
$$\emptyset$$

→   John could not find a viable solution or an answer.
    (Some conjunctions do not come from this sort of rule: e.g., *John and Mary are a nice couple* cannot come from **John is a nice couple and Mary is a nice couple.*)

A rule that is very closely related to Conjunction-reduction is **Gapping**, which deletes identical verbs from predicates which are parallel in structure:

John drinks Scotch and Mary <u>drinks</u> bourbon.

$$\downarrow$$
$$\emptyset$$

→   John drinks Scotch and Mary bourbon.

John tried to reconcile the bank statement and Mary <u>tried to reconcile</u> the checkbook.

$$\downarrow$$
$$\emptyset$$

→   John tried to reconcile the bank statement and Mary the checkbook.

Another rule closely related to Conjunction-reduction is **Reciprocal-formation**, which introduces *each other* into the reduced form of certain conjoined expressions:

John loves Mary, and Mary loves John.
→   John and Mary love each other.

The characteristic that such abbreviatory rules share is that under conditions allowing easy logical recovery based on parallel structure, all repetitive material, all duplication of effort, is cut out. This is one of the two main devices languages use to achieve compactness. The other is to substitute short expressions for longer ones. This is the process of **Anaphoric Substitution**—using part of a phrase, or even special words, as substitutes for the whole longer phrase.

Rules of Anaphora

The best-known kind of anaphora is the substitution of pronouns for NP's. It has been argued that the logic of sentence formation is the other way around; that pronouns are simply the most general names for a class of individuals who are, as it were, selectively spelled out by NP's. Thus the most basic form of a transitive sentence might be like this:

$$\left.\begin{array}{l} \text{He} \\ \text{She} \\ \text{It} \\ \text{They} \\ \text{I} \\ \text{You} \end{array}\right\} \quad \begin{array}{c}\text{Verb} \\ \cdot \\ \cdot \\ \text{hit} \\ \text{hurt} \\ \text{love} \\ \cdot \\ \cdot \end{array} \quad \left\{\begin{array}{l} \text{him} \\ \text{her} \\ \text{it} \\ \text{them} \\ \text{me} \\ \text{you} \end{array}\right.$$

Then any NP that 'spells out' the pronouns more precisely for the speaker can be thought of as being inserted:

He – i.e., the boy I met yesterday – loves *her* – i.e., the girl you told me about.

This proposal has a good deal of appeal, especially since many languages have no obligatory subjects or objects at all, not even pronouns; in some languages the particular agreement affixes of the verb indicate what classes of subjects or objects the speaker has in mind, in a minimal sentence, and these affixes usually derive historically from pronouns. In still other languages, such as Chinese, only context determines the intended subject or object in such sentences.

Whichever may be the better way of looking at the formation of pronouns from NP's, it is clear that, either way, there is an anaphoric relationship between them. For the sake of this discussion, we will speak as though a logical semantic representation existed in which all NP's were fully specified. The relation of pronominal anaphora can then be characterized by a process in which all but one of the NP's which refer to the same individual are replaced by pronouns:

PRONOMINALIZATION

John$_i$ swung the bat at the ball$_j$, but John$_i$ missed the ball$_j$.
(The indices *i, j* indicate identical reference; both *John's* are
the same individual, both *ball's* are the same ball.)
→   John swung the bat at the ball, but *he* missed *it.*

Pronominalization is a vastly more complex process than one might expect. In general, earlier occurrence of two coreferential noun phrases triggers reduction to pronominal form of any subsequent occurrence of that noun phrase (i.e., the rule operates left to right). When, however, there are subordinate clauses, the left-to-right government (the antecedent is the governor, generally to the left) does not hold:

When John$_i$ arrives, send John$_i$ into my office.
→   When John arrives, send him into my office.
(Normal left-to-right government.)
→   When he arrives, send John into my office.
(Antecedent follows pronoun, but is higher in the structure.)

Send John$_i$ into my office when John$_i$ arrives.
→   Send John into my office when he arrives.
↛   *Send him into my office when John arrives.
(Antecedent follows pronoun, but is not higher in the structure, therefore the sentence is ill-formed.)

Rather than always substituting a pronoun for the second (or subordinate) occurrence of an NP, languages often simply delete the one that would be pronominalized, if it is clear what has been deleted. A rule which has this effect in English is known as Equi-NP-deletion, or simply Equi for short:

John persuaded Mary$_i$ (of something) – Mary$_i$ go to the movies with him
$$\downarrow$$
$$\emptyset$$

→   John persuaded Mary to go to the movies with him.

Bill$_i$ was tired (of something) – Bill$_i$ work in a garage
$$\downarrow$$
$$\emptyset$$

→   Bill was tired of working in a garage.

Bill$_i$ repaired cars all day – (Something) gave Bill$_i$ a headache
$$\downarrow$$
$$\emptyset$$

→   Repairing cars all day gave Bill a headache.

Another type of NP-deletion assumes that the relevant NP can be recovered not because it is identical with one that has already appeared in the sentence but because it is implicit in the semantics of the predicate:

INDEFINITE-NP-DELETION

Infrared rays can be lethal to $\begin{cases} \text{one.} \\ \text{a person.} \\ \text{someone.} \end{cases}$
$$\downarrow$$
$$\emptyset$$

→   Infrared rays can be lethal.
LOGIC: they HAVE to be lethal TO someone/something, simply by virtue of the meaning of the predicate *lethal.*

John understands – (the activity of) – $\begin{cases} \text{one} \\ \text{someone} \end{cases}$ skis
$$\downarrow$$
$$\emptyset$$

→   John understands skiing.
LOGIC: *skiing* is an activity; and it must be PERFORMED—it doesn't just HAPPEN.

Most of the devices that natural languages provide for abbreviation of sentence structure operate on the referring expressions; a few, however, operate on the predicates. These are, in effect, PRO-verbs just as forms like *it, he, she* are PRO-nouns. For example:

John tasted the wine, and Mary *tasted the wine, too.*
→   John tasted the wine and *so did* Mary.

Marking for Logical Recovery

But after these focusing and compression devices have worked their destructive way, some restitution must be made if only to give the hearer at least a 50–50 chance of reconstructing the meaning of the sentence, the underlying Logical Form. That is the function of TRACER elements. It is a bit as though we had a sharp, clear blueprint with all the details of a house's construction spelled out explicitly—this is the underlying logical structure. First we shade much of it over with charcoal to make it look more like a house (outlining, as it were, the major features and obliterating details). Then, finding it hard to reconstruct the original drawing, we insert red arrows pointing to crucial details of structure that are still barely perceptible under charcoal shading.

These devices for recovery of the Logical Form differ more from language to language than any of the focusing or compression devices (which, if not universal, are extremely common in a wide range of languages and quite similar in form). The recovery devices differ almost as much as the lexicon and pronunciation, which are the most conspicuous differences between any two languages.

The most common tracer elements in English are the so-called **complementizers** (*for–*)*to*, -*ing*, WH-, and the explicit subordinator *that*. The (*for–*)*to* tracer marks infinitival clauses (details are developed in Chapter VII), which are the reduced form taken, in many cases, by underlying subjunctive clauses:

He ordered *him to leave.*
= . . . that he leave.

It is important *for him to survive.*
= . . . that he survive.

I don't know *how to do it.*
= . . . how one should do it.

The -*ing* tracer marks gerunds of various types:

I don't like his playing the cello.
= I don't like *the fact of* his playing the cello.
    i.e., I don't like the fact that he does it.
= I don't like *the manner of* his playing the cello.
    i.e., I don't like the way that he does it.
= I don't like *the action of* his playing the cello.
    i.e., I don't like for him to do it at all.

Gerunds occur in two distinct configurations, those which have essentially all the properties of ordinary NP's:

His easy swimming of the Hellespont amazed everyone.
    cf. His view of the Hellespont . . .
    His annoyance with the task . . .

and those which seem to lack several of the normal properties of NP's, while retaining somewhat more of the common properties of VP's:

Skiing in Switzerland last year was fun.
I hate slowly burning up every summer.
    cf. We skiied in Switzerland last year.
    I slowly burn up every summer.

The first group have been called 'action nominalizations', from the fact that one of their regular paraphrases is 'the act(ion) of V-*ing*'. They have also been called 'derived nominalizations', from the fact that they are so completely nounlike that they perhaps are best treated along with such verb-derived nouns as *destruction* (from *destroy*), *knowledge* (from *know*), *validation* (from *validate, valid*), all of which have quite similar properties. The second group, which are less NP-like, are then to be viewed as 'true' gerunds, i.e., transformationally related to corresponding atomic sentences. Gerunds are taken up again in Chapter VII.

The WH-tracer primarily marks interrogatives (i.e., it is a trace of the higher sentence *I ask you* . . .). It has also, in the forms *who(m)* and *which*, become a trace of the relative clause:

The boy *who broke his toe* . . .
The idea *which many people rejected* . . .

Explicit Subordinators

When two finite verbs appear in a sentence, there is either a coordination of predicates or a subordination of one to the other. Words like *that*, in

He said *that* he was leaving.

are explicit subordinators. When there is OTHER evidence of subordination (infinitives, gerunds, adverbial markers like *when, while, because*), *that* does not appear in current English, though only a few hundred years ago we said *when that* . . . , *while that* . . . , etc.; i.e., the subordinate marker was more often present with finite verbs in nonmain clauses.

Agreement Rules

We have said a good deal about rules of this type already. Their main function is to mark togetherness, as it were, minimizing the risk that clusters will be wrongly grouped. There is an endless variety of categories of agreement to be found in languages of the world, and the principle is everywhere the same. A head word governs the category membership, and its satellites take on, by copying-rules, markings which identify them as belonging to that head. Classes that commonly agree are these:

HEAD	SATELLITE
N	ADJ
N	DET
N	QUANT
SUBJ	Finite Verb
NP (antecedent)	Pronoun
Higher V	Lower V

Reflexivization

Most languages provide a means of marking coreferentiality up to a point. English marks it only up through a single clause:

John$_i$ hurt John$_i$.
→   John hurt himself.
John$_i$ hurt someone else.
→   John hurt him.

John said   he   was leaving.

John   someone else

↛   *John said himself was leaving.

That is, beyond the boundary of a single clause, English has no automatic way of expressing coreferentiality. Other languages are more expressive in this respect:

Ojo   ro   pe   ón   mu   sasa.   (Yoruba)
Ojo$_i$ thinks   that   he$_i$ is   smart
Ojo thinks that he (himself) is smart.

Ojo   ro   pe   ŏ   mu   sasa.
Ojo$_i$ thinks   that   he$_j$ is   smart
Ojo thinks that he (someone else) is smart.

John luuli että $\left\{ \begin{array}{c} \emptyset \\ h\ddot{a}n \end{array} \right\}$ *oli sairas.*   (Finnish)

John$_i$ thought that $\left\{ \begin{array}{c} he_i \\ he_j \end{array} \right\}$ was sick.

Dummy Fillers (Slot Holders)

Languages which have well-marked person–number affixes in verbs may omit subjects which are transparent in the context or in verbal affixes:

Estoy saliendo.   (Spanish)
am   leaving
I am leaving.

In languages where the verbal marking of subjects is less conspicuous, the inclusion of SOME stipulated subject may become obligatory. The obligatoriness may then extend into contexts where no REAL subject makes sense. Consider the difference between Spanish and English:

> *Está lloviendo.*
> is   raining
> It's raining.

What is the *it* of English? What is raining? The weather? Cats and dogs? The clouds? *It*, in this usage, is a mere dummy to fill the subject slot.

Summary

To paraphrase what Donne said about the compass, of which one leg returns to where it 'begun', it is time to return to where we begun, too, with an example that was intended to arouse curiosity in Chapter I:

> *I don't know where Bill's.

Why can't *Bill is* be contracted in this sort of sentence? It certainly can be elsewhere:

> Bill's at the movies.
> Bill's working.
> Bill's over there.
> I know Bill's tired.
> .
> .
> .

The underlying structure of this sentence is, roughly and not even very abstractly:

> I don't know – Bill is at WH-some place

WH-fronting (a focusing rule) moves *at WH-some place* to the front of its clause. This gives:

> I don't know – at – WH-some place Bill is

By low-level spelling rules, we have:

> I don't know – at what place Bill is
>   ↓
>   where

It is clear that a constituent has been moved OUT from the position immediately following the copulative verb. Whenever this happens— whenever COP loses its immediate rightside neighbor—contraction cannot apply in English. (There are other examples with contracted *have* and with reduced prepositional forms that work the same way.) We now have a description that correctly predicts the conditions under which reduction (contraction) will and won't occur. But we have no explanation; we do not know why this constraint on reduction should hold, even though it apparently DOES hold with perfect consistency. There are other phenomena all over the syntactic map which are in exactly this status, or the converse of it; we have a reasonable explanation of the logical structure of a construction such as the comparative, but no set of rules which will account precisely for the variety of grammatical forms, while excluding the ungrammatical ones of that language. In very few cases for very few languages are BOTH the conditions of well-formedness and the conditions on semantic interpretation adequately described over any significant range of data. With that rather depressing observation, we turn to a discussion of the nature of evidence in syntactic theory.

Evidence in Syntax

Any rule of a grammar is a hypothesis about some aspect of what a class of well-formed sentences looks like, and about some aspect of how those sentences are interpreted. That is, grammatical rules make two kinds of predictions: predictions about **form** and predictions about **meaning**. The quality of the predictions must be measured, therefore, by at least these two conditions of adequacy: (A) Do the predicted sentences agree with judgments made by native speakers about the form of such sentences? Are such forms fully grammatical? Marginally acceptable? Grammatically deviant in some readily identifiable respect? Totally unacceptable? (B) Do the predicted meanings agree with the way such sentences are understood by native speakers? Are the sentences ambiguous in the ways predicted? Are they correct (partial or full) paraphrases of some other sentence(s)? Do they correctly entail or imply the meanings of other sentences?

The evidence that is relevant to evaluating hypotheses with respect to these conditions of adequacy is relatively accessible, although from its accessibility one cannot conclude that it is also readily interpretable. At this stage in the history of linguistic theory there is almost never a UNIQUE hypothesis that makes all the correct predictions. Usually there are SEVERAL hypotheses, mutually incompatible, which make many of the correct predictions, but which fail in either of two directions:

1. They leak; i.e., they fail to make all the necessary predictions (they don't cover all the relevant data).
2. They balloon; i.e., they cover all the relevant data, but they go too far and make additional predictions which are incorrect.

The incessant leaking and ballooning of grammatical rules has stimulated scholars through centuries of research to try to find better ways to formulate grammars. Through such research enough solid knowledge about the nature of human language has been accumulated to add a third condition of adequacy on the formulation of grammatical rules: (C) Is the rule formulated in a way that would be possible or meaningful also for other languages? Is the rule formulated in accord with established GENERAL properties, TYPOLOGICAL characteristics, of natural languages?

Finally, individual grammatical rules are evaluated (D) in relation to the other rules that together make up a total grammar. This is a matter of internal consistency and simplicity, and although it is highly prized by the in-group adherents of particular warring camps of grammarians, it is the least accessible to evaluation or appreciation from outside.

In the sections which follow here, some typical claims about grammatical rules are exemplified, with a summary of some of the pieces of evidence—(A) formal, (B) semantic, (C) typological, and (D) system-internal—that can be cited for and against these claims. The claims that are cited are relatively narrow and modest ones, extracted in an unrepresentative way from various rich traditions of syntactic analysis, and the evidence cited is of course very fragmentary. The intent is to provide a feel for what sort of evidence is relevant, rather than to exhaust ANY argument.

Subjects of Imperative Verbs

English sentences like the following have the unusual property that they lack any NP to serve as subject of the verb:

Leave me alone.
Go outside and play with your friends.
Behave yourself.

They are traditionally said to have an 'understood' subject *you*. That traditional claim is essentially a statement of the semantic evidence: imperative sentences are indeed interpreted just as they would be interpreted if there were an expressed subject *you:*

> You leave me alone.
> You go outside and play with your friends.
> You behave yourself.

This semantic evidence is made explicit with the observation that only the pronoun *you* can refer BACK to the subject of imperative sentences, as in the second example above, where *your friends* can refer only to the *you* that is understood to be the subject of *Go outside and play....*

The semantic evidence is supported by two pieces of formal evidence. (1) The form of the reflexive pronoun shows that there must be a subject *you* to explain why the reflexive is *yourself* rather than some other form (it has to agree with the subject in person and number):

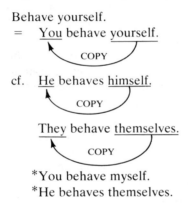

> *You behave myself.
> *He behaves themselves.

(2) The form of tag questions is also evidence because such questions must contain pronoun copies of the subject of the main verb to which the tag refers:

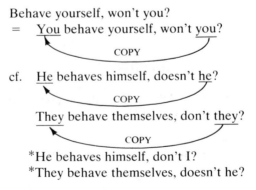

> *He behaves himself, don't I?
> *They behave themselves, doesn't he?

Higher Verb 'Command'

Besides the fact that imperative sentences evidently have a subject *you* that is present in the underlying form (the Logical Form or semantic representation) and deleted in the course of derivation to the surface form, these sentences differ from others notably also in the fact that their verb cannot take any auxiliary verb:

> Leave me alone.
> *Can leave me alone.
> *Will leave me alone.
> *Have left me alone.
> *Be leaving me alone.

Semantically, there is some not altogether persuasive support for the claim that all imperative sentences are understood to contain a future auxiliary (*will*) which is deleted, along with the subject *you*, in the course of derivation:

> YOU WILL leave me alone   →   Leave me alone.

There is some formal support, too, for this suggestion. (1) The form of the imperative verb in English is identical to the form that occurs with *will* (the infinitive form without *to*). (2) Tag questions, which always contain a copy of the auxiliary verb and subject of the main clause, with the negation reversed, suggest an underlying *will*:

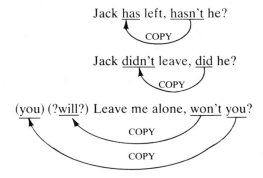

However, the tag question on the imperative can be formed equally well with at least one other auxiliary:

> Leave me alone, can't you?

The tag does not have to reverse the negative polarity of the main verb, in the imperative:

Leave me alone, $\left\{\begin{array}{l}\text{will} \\ \text{won't}\end{array}\right\}$ you?

In short, the proposal that imperatives have an underlying *will* does not make the correct formal predictions. Furthermore, the semantics of the claim is highly suspect; while it is true that commands imply some sort of futurity, the meaning of simple future assertions is very different from that of commands:

> You will leave me alone.
> (A prediction about the future: the speaker claims that in some future time, this will be the state of affairs.)

> Leave me alone.
> (A request/command that this SHOULD BECOME the future state of affairs.)

The foregoing evidence considerably weakens the claim that imperatives should be derived from corresponding assertions. An alternative proposal is that they should be derived from sentences of the form:

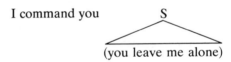

This proposal has some virtues. Semanticially it precisely captures the fact that all imperatives entail a first-person speaker, and a second-person addressee (*I . . . you*). It does not suggest identity with future assertions, but instead derives its future sense from the natural semantic implication that a command can be executed only at a point in time subsequent to the command itself. Formally, the proposal provides an explanation for the disappearance of the imperative subject *you*, by making use of the general rule of Equi-NP-deletion, some aspects of which we saw earlier (Chapters V and VI):

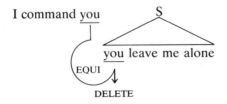

Having deleted the subject from the lower sentence by Equi, we have two options, both of which are formally parallel to processes elsewhere in the grammar. We can apply the rules which turn a lower verb into infinitival form:

> I command you – *to* – leave me alone.
>> cf.   I asked him *to* leave me alone.
>> I persuaded Mary *to* leave.

Or we can delete the entire upper structure, leaving the normal imperative form:

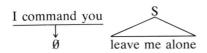

This proposal, therefore, has good formal, semantic, and internal support. It also has some typological support, namely the fact that in many languages the special form of the verb that appears in the lower sentence ('subjunctive' in western European grammars, for example) is identical to or obviously closely related to the form of the imperative, as in this Spanish example:

> *Mando*   *que*   ***salga***   *usted*   *ahora*   *mismo.*
> command-I   that   leave-SUBJUNC   you   now   same
> I command that you leave right now.
>
>> cf.   *Dice*   *que*   ***sale***   *usted*   *ahora*   *mismo.*
>>   says-he   that   leave   you   now   same
>>   He says that you are leaving right now.
>
> ***salga***   *usted*   *ahora*   *mismo.*
> leave-IMPER   you   now   same
> Leave right now!

In the above example, compare the forms *salga* and *sale*. *Salga* occurs in the subordinate clause after a verb meaning 'I command', and it is exactly the same form that is used in the direct command. The other form, *sale*, is used in subordinate clauses where there is only a sense of reporting, not commanding (or the like), in the higher verb: and this is the indicative form of the verb that is used in ordinary declarative sentences.

Presentative *there*

There is no fully satisfactory analysis of sentences like these:

There's a snake in the garden.
There's a concert at two o'clock.
There're plenty of good cellists in the world.

It is widely assumed that they should be derived from simple sentences like these:

A snake is in the garden.
A concert is at two o'clock.
Plenty of good cellists are in the world.

One serious problem of this proposal is that these supposedly more basic sentences are highly questionable; while they may not be totally unacceptable, they are at the very least so unnatural as to suggest that they violate some sort of grammatical constraint. Notice how much better the same sentences are if the subject-NP is definite:

The snake is in the garden.
The concert is at two o'clock.
The world has plenty of good cellists.

It's clear that the function of *there* is pragmatic: it introduces new expressions into the discourse, assigning a reference to them which is thereafter shared by hearer and speaker. At the same time, it obviously is not an NP subject in the usual sense, even though it precedes the verb in declarative sentences, since it does not control agreement with the verb:

$$\text{There} \left\{ \begin{array}{l} \textit{is} \text{ a snake} \\ \textit{are} \text{ some snakes} \end{array} \right\} \text{ in the garden.}$$

Formally, it looks like the ADV *there* 'in that place', but it is quite different from the adverb in several crucial ways. (1) It is unstressed, whereas the adverb, when in front of the verb, is heavily stressed:

ADV
There is another firecracker.

                          ADV
There is another firecracker *there* in the drawer.

(2) The meaning of the ADV *there* can be precisely captured by the paraphrase 'in that place':

> There
> In that place } you can find another firecracker.

whereas 'in that place' is totally unacceptable as a paraphrase of the presentative *there:*

> *In that place is another firecracker there in the drawer.

Typologically, the presentative construction takes a wide variety of forms, even among languages related to English such as German, Spanish, and French:

> **Es gibt** *hier* *ein* *Problem.* (German)
> it   gives   here   a   problem
> There is a problem here.

> **Hay** *un* *problema* *aquí.* (Spanish)
> has   a   problem   here
> There is a problem here.

> **Il** *y* **a** *un* *problème* *ici.* (French)
> it   there   has   a   problem   here
> There is a problem here.

In some other languages there is a word for the presentative function which has no other meaning, as in the following Tagalog examples:

> *May* *problema.*
> exists   problem
> There is a problem.

> *Mayroon* *problema.*
> exists-not   problem
> There is no problem.

Although these various types of evidence do not converge on an obvious analysis, they generally support the view that the presentative formula (whatever shape it takes in a particular language) is a sort of 'existence' predicate, equivalent, in many ways, to the symbol ∃ in logic:

> $\exists x P(x) =$ 'There exists an x, such that P is true of that x.'

In a simplified tree-diagram, using the example *There's a snake in the garden:*

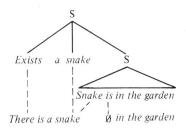

Reflexives

Since the early days of transformational grammar, it has been widely accepted that sentences like

John hurt himself.

are to be analyzed as deriving from an underlying structure that contains two occurrences of a referentially identical NP:

John$_i$ hurt John$_i$.

This analysis claims that in all essential semantic respects, *John hurt himself* is like

John hurt Bill.

and that the second occurrence of *John$_i$* is replaced by *himself* under quite general rules of pronoun formation:

John$_i$ hurt John$_i$
                    ↓
               himself

Formally, this claim is supported by at least two facts. (1) The reflexive forms appear to be related to other pronouns—*him/himself, her/herself, them/themselves, it/itself*—but this formal relation is offset by the fact that the other reflexive pronouns do not in fact correspond with the ordinary object pronouns, but rather with possessives: *me/myself, you/yourself, us/ourselves.* Indeed, the nonstandard forms *hisself, theirselves* suggest that the possessive forms may be more basic. (2) The -*self* forms appear to be nouns, in that they have nounlike singular/plural forms.

In other formal respects, the claim does not fare so well: reflexive pronouns cannot occur in several functions where ordinary pronouns and NP's can:

SUBJECT

> John hurt himself.
> *Himself was hurt by John.
>   cf.   John hurt Bill.
>   Bill was hurt by John.

POSSESSIVE

> John$_i$ broke John's$_i$ arm.
> *John broke himself's arm.

RELATIVE PRONOUN

> The boy who likes her best is handsome.
> *The boy whoself likes her best is handsome.

CONJUNCTION

> John and Mary hurt John and Mary.
> *John and Mary hurt himself and herself.

But much more damaging are the semantic considerations. Consider what the semantic consequences are if we add a quantifier like *only* to an ordinary transitive sentence:

> John hurt Bill.
> Only John hurt Bill.
> =   No one except John hurt Bill.

Now we attach the same quantifier to a transitive reflexive:

> Only John hurt himself.

This—surprisingly, and WRONGLY if the proposed analysis is correct—does not mean

> No one except John hurt John.

but rather

> No one except John got hurt.

Similarly, a construction like the following implies that Mary hurt Bill:

> John hurt Bill, and so did Mary.

But the corresponding reflexive construction—again surprisingly, and WRONGLY if the proposed analysis is correct—does not imply that Mary hurt Bill, but that Mary hurt herself:

Bill hurt himself, and so did Mary.

Typologically, the proposed analysis is a disaster; NOT A SINGLE LANGUAGE known to contemporary scholarship expresses the reflexive notion by actually repeating the subject in object position.

While the foregoing discussion provides evidence that the standard analysis is wrong, it is more difficult to set forth an adequate alternative.[1] At the very least, an alternative should provide for the fact that 'verb + oneself' is somehow a UNIT, like a single intransitive verb, in order to explain the fact that, for example,

John killed himself and Mary did, too.

can only mean that both Mary and John committed suicide, rather than meaning that Mary contributed to the killing of John. Typologically, at least, such a notion of **reflexive verb** is widespread.

Raising (to Subject)

Raising rules (abbreviated RAIS) have come into earlier discussions throughout this book; all languages, as far as we know, have Raising rules of one type or another, and they serve extremely important pragmatic functions (Chapter VI). We will consider, here, some of the specific justifications[2] for claiming that such rules exist in English.

One class of examples of Raising appears in pairs of sentences like these:

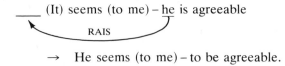

    →   He seems (to me) – to be agreeable.

---

[1] Keenan (1972) provides a full discussion of three alternatives.

[2] Postal (1974) provides the fullest, and most stimulating, study of this topic yet undertaken. It is not, however, accessible to the beginning student. The following discussion is so superficial, compared with Postal's, that I hesitate to refer to his work at all; nevertheless, much of what follows here is directly due to his study.

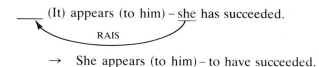

(It) appears (to him) – she has succeeded.

RAIS

→   She appears (to him) – to have succeeded.

The relevant semantic intuition is that the members of each pair are synonymous; i.e., in both instances there is an assertion that such-and-such a proposition *seems/appears* (to someone, namely the speaker) to be true:

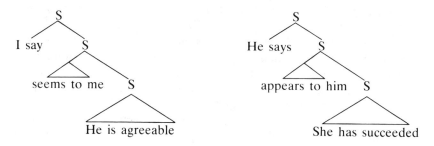

This semantic intuition, which is formalized by assigning only a single semantic representation to each pair, can be tested in various ways. For instance, do the two forms remain semantically constant under some additional semantic function like negation? Yes, they do:

It does *not* appear that she has succeeded.
=   She does *not* appear to have succeeded.

Do the two forms remain semantically constant under some additional semantic function like quantification? Yes, again:

It seems to me that *only* he is agreeable.
=   *Only* he seems to me to be agreeable.

But the basic evidence is simply truth equivalence. If one is false, the other should be, within each pair; and conversely, if one is true, the other should also be. And that is correct, as the reader can readily verify for himself.

Semantically, then, the claim is well supported. Formally, there is also good support. Consider sentences which have dummy subjects:

It's raining.
There's a snake in the garden.

With *seem*, these occur in two forms:

> It seems (that) it's raining.
> It seems to be raining.

> It seems (that) there's a snake in the garden.
> There seems to be a snake in the garden.

We saw earlier that the presentative *there* can be argued to be derived from a higher predicate operating on a sentence with a nondefinite subject. If that is correct, then there would be no source for the *there* which appears in *There seems to be a snake in the garden* except for it to have been raised from the lower clause *There's a snake in the garden.* In examples like *It's raining*, the *it* can be argued to have no function except to occupy the subject position in front of the verb (this is a characteristic of languages which are now verb-second languages, like German, and of languages which once were verb-second even though, like English, they have become verb-medial, having the verb after the subject, but not necessarily second). If this is correct, so that verbs like *rain, snow, thunder, storm,* etc. are simply zero-place predications about the existence of the event named by the corresponding noun, the *it* of *It seems to be raining* would have no source except to have been raised from the dummy subject slot of the lower clause:

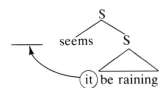

It seems to be raining.

One might argue, however, that the *it* of this construction is ANOTHER dummy *it*, which shows up in

> *It* seems that it is raining.

and then, one could claim, the *it* of the lower clause is deleted by Equi:

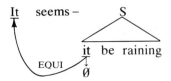

Although this would work, for this example, it would mean that dummy *it* must be generated all over the grammar, wherever any NP can occur, creating an enormous ballooning of ungrammaticalness or meaninglessness:

> It wants to leave.   (*It* as in *It rained.*)
> I found it.   (*It* as in *I found it to be raining.*)

The nature of this chaos can be appreciated more fully perhaps by noting other highly restricted idiomatic subjects:

> Not much heed is paid to his muttering.
> Not much heed seems to be paid to his muttering.

Since (*not much*) *heed* exists only as an underlying object of *pay* in the idiom *pay* NEG *heed,* there is no way to get it as the subject of *seem* except through this sequence of steps:

SOURCE: Seems – No one pays much heed to his muttering.
PASSIVE: Seems – Not much heed is paid (by anyone) to his muttering.
RAISING: Not much heed seems to be paid (by anyone) to his muttering.

If, contrary to this derivation, we assume that *not much heed* can be simply an ordinary NP subject of any verb, including *seem,* then the grammar will balloon to allow such ungrammatical forms as the following:

> *Not much heed bothered him.
> *Not much heed seemed to bother him.

> *Not much heed is needed in the world.
> *Not much heed seems to be needed in the world.

Notice that some of the preceding arguments are grammar-internal. If you make certain assumptions about *it, there,* and *pay heed,* then certain consequences follow for the analysis of Raising. It is virtually impossible to look at a single rule in isolation.

Raising (to Object)

In all examples of Raising-to-subject, the sentence from which the Raising took place functioned itself as the LOGICAL SUBJECT of the higher verb:

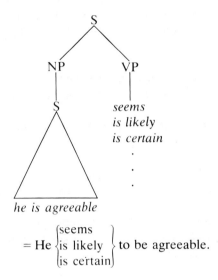

$$= \text{He} \begin{Bmatrix} \text{seems} \\ \text{is likely} \\ \text{is certain} \end{Bmatrix} \text{to be agreeable.}$$

Similarly, all examples of Raising-to-object lift the subject of a sentence which is functioning as LOGICAL OBJECT up into the nominal object position immediately after the higher verb:

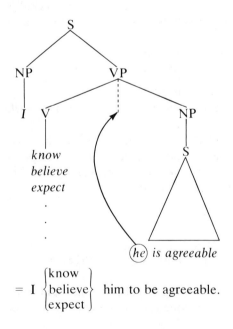

$$= \text{I} \begin{Bmatrix} \text{know} \\ \text{believe} \\ \text{expect} \end{Bmatrix} \text{him to be agreeable.}$$

The reader may see for himself that several of the arguments for Raising-to-subject carry over, essentially unchanged, to this analysis:

SYNONYMY

I believe³ $\begin{cases} \text{(that) he is agreeable.} \\ \text{him to be agreeable.} \end{cases}$

DUMMY SUBJECTS

I believe $\begin{cases} \text{(that) it is raining.} \\ \text{it to be raining.} \end{cases}$

I expect $\begin{cases} \text{(that) there will be opposition.} \\ \text{there to be opposition.} \end{cases}$

IDIOMATICITY

I believe $\begin{cases} \text{(that) little heed was paid to his ideas.} \\ \text{little heed to have been paid to his ideas.} \end{cases}$

But none of these arguments actually prove that the subject of the lower sentence has been converted into an object of the higher verb. Similar examples are persuasive for Raising-to-subject, but not for Raising-to-object, because in the former case the subject of the lower clause is PHYSICALLY separated from its verb, and indeed can be separated by several intervening verbs, being raised in successive steps:

There is certain to appear to be a problem with catalytic converters.

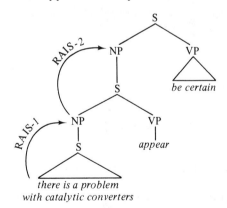

there is a problem
with catalytic converters

³ Other verbs like *believe* are *understand, think, know, discover, consider, claim, find.* A slightly different group of verbs is represented by *expect,* which requires a future sense in its object clause:

I expect $\begin{cases} \text{that he will be agreeable.} \\ \text{him to be agreeable.} \end{cases}$

Since this kind of separation is not possible in the examples of Raising-to-object, one must determine whether there is evidence to show that some sort of sentential boundary exists between the newly raised object of the higher verb and the lower verb that was its erstwhile mate. One way to show that such a boundary exists is by demonstrating that the raised object can participate in rules which are known (on other evidence) to be restricted to the domain of a single clause. One such rule is Passive, which promotes an object to subject and demotes the subject to an oblique case (or deletes it):

PASSIVE

>   Everyone believes the Bible.
> $\xrightarrow{\text{PASS}}$ The Bible is believed by everyone.

This rule will not promote the subject of a lower sentence:

>   Everyone believes $_S$[the Bible is infallible].
> $\xrightarrow{\text{PASS}}\!\!\!\!/$ *The Bible is believed is infallible (by everyone).

But if the subject of the lower sentence has been raised to object of the higher verb, then the Passive rule applies normally:

>   Everyone believes the Bible is infallible.
> $\xrightarrow{\text{RAIS}}$ Everyone believes the Bible to be infallible.
> $\xrightarrow{\text{PASS}}$ The Bible is believed to be infallible (by everyone).

Another rule that is restricted to the domain of a single clause is the one discussed earlier which forms reflexive pronouns:

REFLEXIVE

>   John$_i$ believes John$_i$.
> $\xrightarrow{\text{REFL}}$ John believes himself.

It will not reflexivize the subject of a lower sentence:

>   John$_i$ believes John$_i$ is infallible.
> $\xrightarrow{\text{REFL}}\!\!\!\!/$ *John believes himself is infallible.

But if the subject of the lower sentence has been raised to object of the higher verb, then reflexivization is permitted:

>   John$_i$ believes John$_i$ is infallible.
> $\xrightarrow{\text{RAIS}}$ John$_i$ believes John$_i$ to be infallible.
> $\xrightarrow{\text{RAIS}}$ John believes himself to be infallible.

A similar argument exists for the formation of reciprocal pronouns:

John$_i$ and Mary$_j$ believe John$_i$ and Mary$_j$ are infallible.[4]
$\xrightarrow{\text{RECIP}}$ *John and Mary believe each other are infallible.
John and Mary believe John and Mary are infallible.
$\xrightarrow{\text{RAIS}}$ John and Mary believe John and Mary to be infallible.
$\xrightarrow{\text{RECIP}}$ John and Mary believe each other to be infallible.

It is obvious that the preceding arguments for Raising-to-object depend to a large extent on system-internal considerations. By changing certain assumptions about the way in which the domain of a rule's applicability is determined, all three of these arguments can be weakened. The arguments are only as persuasive as other aspects of the theory within which they are embedded. As far as we know at this time, there is no evidence external to particular theories which would support or invalidate the Raising analysis; i.e., the correct formal and semantic predictions can be made, for these sentences, in ways other than the ones favored above. Within this theory, however, the system-internal arguments of the type outlined above are quite strong, and they are reinforced by general arguments for Infinitive-formation that are outlined below.

Infinitive Formation

In discussing tracer elements (Chapter VI), we noted that the raised version of sentences contains an **Infinitive** form of the verb in the lower sentence (i.e., a verbal form marked by the tracer element *to*). Raised subjects invariably leave behind predicates that must be changed to infinitival form:

John seems *to be agreeable.*
    cf. It seems that John *is agreeable.*
    *John seems *is agreeable.*
They believe John *to be infallible.*
    cf. They believe that John *is infallible.*

Another syntactic rule which leaves behind predicates that must change to infinitival form is Equi-NP-deletion, a rule which we have seen in

---

[4] Actually this is much oversimplified. The deeper structure of reciprocals is something like *John believes Mary is infallible, and Mary believes John is infallible.*

operation earlier (Chapters V and VI):

John$_i$ wants – John$_i$ leave
    EQUI   DELETE

→ John wants to leave.

John persuaded Mary$_i$ – Mary$_i$ leave
            EQUI   DELETE

→ John persuaded Mary to leave.

It is important for John$_i$ – John$_i$ leave
             EQUI   DELETE

→ It is important for John to leave.

John$_i$ works at night – in order (that) – John$_i$ make more money
                       EQUI   DELETE

→ John works at night in order to make more money.

It is easy for one – one go broke
            EQUI   DELETE

→ It is easy for one – to go broke.
            DELETE
            INDEF NP

→ It is easy – to go broke.

I didn't ask – how one can solve the problem.
            DELETE
            INDEF NP

→ I didn't ask – how to solve the problem.

The interesting question is this: why does the rule of Infinitive-formation apply in just these kinds of sentences? What do they have in common that would explain why infinitives arise in precisely these circumstances? Is it some semantic feature they share? Is it quite accidental; i.e., is there really no generalization to be found at all, but merely a list of types of constructions that call for infinitives? Is it some formal feature, something about the phrase-marker of exactly THESE sentence types, something about the surface signaling devices, that calls for a special form of the verb?

The most insightful answer that we have found in the literature[5] is that infinitives are introduced whenever, for any reason, there is no subject for the verb to agree with. There are two conditions under which this commonly occurs: it is deleted (as by Equi-NP-deletion or Indefinite-NP-deletion in the examples above), or it is raised out of the sentence in which its own verb appears.[6] Inspection of the examples above will show that **subject–verb agreement** cannot be applied on the lower verb after its subject has been either deleted or raised. The specific effect of Infinitive-formation is then to delete that part of the lower verb phrase which marks the tense and modality of the predicate, and to insert the tracer element *to* at the head of the rest of the verb phrase:

He_i expects – he_i will leave
EQUI: He expects – $\emptyset$ will leave
INF: He expects – to $\emptyset$ leave

It is important for $Mary_i$ – $Mary_i$ will have left before midnight
EQUI: It is important for Mary – $\emptyset$ will have left before midnight
INF: It is important for Mary –   to $\emptyset$ have left before midnight

This analysis strongly supports the analysis of Raising-to-object since it captures within a single generalization an explanation of Infinitive-formation in all raised structures—one which is totally lost if either Raising-to-subject or Raising-to-object is analyzed in some way which fails to dissociate the raised NP from its verb (since it is this dissociation which blocks subject–verb agreement in a natural way).

Gerund Formation

There are several types of gerunds in English, and a great deal can be said about different analyses of them. Here we want to concentrate on only one aspect of gerunds; namely, under what syntactic or semantic conditions are gerunds formed (rather than finite verbs or infinitives)? What is it that forces, or allows, Gerundivization in these sets?

---

[5] In Kiparsky and Kiparsky (1970).
[6] The Kiparskys proposed certain other conditions for loss of subject (by Accusative-marking) which are less persuasive; in the examples above, these types are reformulated as additional instances of Equi applying to datives (*for*-phrases).

Their having played Bartok annoyed him.   GERUND
    cf. *They played Bartok annoyed him.   FINITE
         For them to have played Bartok annoyed him.   INFINITIVE

He acknowledged having studied the fugue.
    cf. *He acknowledged to have studied the fugue.
         He acknowledged (that) he had studied the fugue.

He avoids working if he can.
    cf. *He avoids to work if he can.
         *He avoids that he works if he can.

Hunting tigers is fun.
    cf. *One hunts tigers is fun.
         ?For one to hunt tigers is fun.

Without admitting it, they reformed.
    cf. *Without they admitted it, they reformed.
         *Without to admit it, they reformed.
         *Without for them to admit it, they reformed.

They went hunting.
    cf. *They went (that) they hunt.
         They went to hunt.   (Okay as purpose clause only, not as
                                  a paraphrase of *They went hunting*.)

It is assumed, in accord with the general principle that we have maintained throughout, that surface gerunds must reflect full propositions in
the logical structure, propositions that are amalgamated with other propositions to form complex sentences in which the gerund -*ing* forms are
tracer elements that signal on the surface some particular types of
subordination in the logical structures of messages. For evidence about
what these logical structures are, we look to paraphrases. Among examples with gerunds, we can discern two distinct semantic classes:

1. FACTIVES (the subordinate predicate is presupposed by the speaker to
      be true):

Their having played Bartok annoyed him.
=   (The fact of) their having played Bartok ...
=   (The fact) that they played Bartok ...

He acknowledged having studied the fugue.
=   ... (the fact of) having studied ...
=   ... (the fact) that he had studied ...

2. ACTIONS (the subordinate predicate expresses an action that the
    speaker makes some assertion about):

He avoids working if he can.
=   ... (the act(ion) of) working ...

Hunting tigers is fun.
=   (The act(ion) of) hunting tigers is fun.

But besides these two classes, there are examples which do not lend
themselves to a semantic characterization. The last two above are not
obviously either factive or actional:

Without admitting it, they reformed.
≠   Without the fact of admitting it, ...
≠   Without the action of admitting it, ...

They went hunting.
≠   They went (on) the fact of hunting.
≠   They went (on) the action of hunting.

Rather, it appears that in the simple prepositional example, we would like
the analysis merely to express the fact that *without* is followed by a
sentential object:

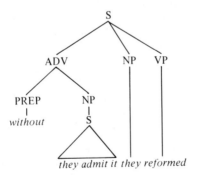

The last example (*They went hunting*) is more difficult: *hunting* is some
sort of adverb, it would seem, perhaps like the phrase *at it* in

They went *at it* hammer and tongs.
They went (*at*) *hunting*.

The question, then, is this: What, if anything, do these two semantic
classes ('factive' and 'actional') have in common with the adverbial types,
such that all of them are formed with gerunds? HYPOTHESIS: Since in all

the sets above, at least one version of each sentence has a preposition governing the gerund, perhaps we can conclude that the gerund is simply that form which verbs take as they become nounlike in function. In other words, the tracer function of the *-ing* affix that marks gerunds is to say that the SEMANTICALLY predicational element to which it is attached (the verb) is FORMALLY occupying a role which is typical of nouns, not of verbs (i.e., in these cases, it is the object of a preposition). To maintain this hypothesis, we must maintain that at some level of representation, every gerund is governed by a preposition. The preposition, in turn, must be deleted in the course of the derivation of some of the paraphrastic forms of the sentences in question, as indicated by parentheses in the sets above.

Conclusion:
A Note on the Recent History
of Syntactic Theory

It is one of the verities of science that no empirical hypothesis can ever be proved to be correct. It can only be proved wrong (and even that accomplishment is rare). It is also a verity, or nearly so, that a scientific bird in the hand is worth two in the bush. That is, scholars will cling tenaciously to an explanation, or a principle, or a 'law', that they know to be wrong, because they do not have in hand an alternative explanation which is clearly better in the two crucial ways that it MUST be better: (1) it must cover the same range of facts, or an enlarged range of facts, and (2) it must do so more simply, more satisfyingly in some sense that is ultimately esthetic, than the hypothesis currently in use.

A particular mode of explanation, a particular set of principles and laws, a particular frame of reference, within a discipline is known as a 'paradigm' for work in that field. The paradigm determines the questions that are of interest, the kinds of evidence that are accepted as persuasive, the kinds of argumentation that prevail at scholarly meetings and in scholarly publication, and—ultimately—who talks to whom, within the field. If there are distinct and incompatible paradigms in existence, a scholar who is committed to one may be quite blind to the insights of work that is performed within a different paradigm, and conversely.

This chapter has dealt superficially with the notion 'evidence' in a theory of syntax. But of course what constitutes evidence, even what constitutes a question, must vary between paradigms. At this time in the history of linguistics (approximately the American Bicentennial), the status of alternative paradigms is not as clear as it was. While the classical transformational paradigm of Chomsky (1965) still dominates many major university departments of linguistics, there are two distinct movements away from that classical position: (1) a move in the direction of assigning ever greater weight to semantic evidence, with the result that the objectives of syntactic theory become inseparable from the general goal of explaining the logical Semantic Structure of language; and (2) a move away from assigning to syntactic analysis any significant role in the explanation of meaning, confining its task to that of distinguishing between well-formed and ill-formed strings of words in the language, while characterizing semantic interpretation by independent devices. The split, oversimplified, is between semantic function and formal structure, which we have tried in this book to see as twin prongs of the same thrust. And coexisting, not always tranquilly, with the Chomskyan paradigm and its two lines of divergent development, are several important theories which have not been touched upon here at all. We have dealt with the kinds of facts, and the kinds of explanatory notions, that we believe all theories must handle under some similar set of assumptions. The differences, we hope, will increasingly turn out to be matters of notation and terminology.

Acknowledgments

GENERAL

    I cannot hope to make these complete. I have tried to list here those SPECIFIC debts that I am aware of, as distinct from those which I have accumulated at a great rate merely by virtue of participating in the normal pursuits of an academic career in my field. As far as I know for sure, NOTHING in the entire book is original with me; but nothing beyond what is acknowledged below and in the text itself was knowingly taken from a particular source uniquely recoverable as to name, time, or place. That is, whatever remains unacknowledged is my own synthesis of widely available information and ideas, as far as I am aware.

CHAPTER I

    I owe the examples and interpretation of English contraction to King (1970); the example of agreement failure determining semantic interpretation to Robert Kirsner (personal communication); the analysis of copular sentences to Hutchins (1971); the notion 'kernel' or 'atomic' sentence to

Harris (1952, 1957); the parallelism between semantic and syntactic constraints, on the one hand, to articulatory universals and phonological constraints, on the other, to Martin Joos (personal communication); the observations about extraction of WH-words from headed clauses to Ross (1967); the analysis of Raising to Kiparsky and Kiparsky (1970) and Postal (1974).

CHAPTER II

I owe the terms 'entity word' versus 'event word' to Bull (1960); the relation of categorial distinctions to logical forms to Vennemann (1973a); the Navajo example to Sanford Schane (personal communication); the analysis of tense/aspect functions to Bull (1960); the recognition of the importance of topic/comment functions, scattered throughout the book, to many pleasant hours with Theo Vennemann and Talmy Givón, several of whose works are listed in the bibliography; several key notions about adverbs to Bartsch (1972); the relation of the predicate *use* to instrumental adverbs to Lakoff (1968); the hierarchy of noun features to Nilsen (1970); the notion of 'rank-shifting' to Halliday (1961); the notion of 'common focus' to Bull (1960); the importance of NP's as independently referring expressions to Keenan (1972); the analysis of parallelism between noun plus complement and verb plus complement (here and in Chapter III) to Chomsky (1970) and to Stockwell, Schachter, and Partee (1973); the notion of case-affixes and pre/postpositions as higher predicates to Hetzron (1974); the identification of cases with pre/postpositions to Fillmore (1966).

CHAPTER III

I owe the Persian examples to Galust Madirussian (personal communication); the Tagalog examples to Schachter and Otanes (1972); the 'married happily' example to Pope (1971); all references to Behaghel (first law, second law), whose work I have not read, to Theo Vennemann in personal communications and in several of his publications; the Japanese examples to Katsue Akiba and to Edward Finegan (personal communications); the German examples to Vennemann (forthcoming a). The generalizations about SOV, SVO, VSO languages are due originally to Greenberg (1963a), as developed by Lehmann (1973) and Vennemann (1973b). The Chinese examples I owe to Sandra Thompson (personal communication) and to Li and Thompson (1975). The discussion of what makes a 'good' inflectional system is based on the views of Vennemann as found in his 1973 papers and especially in Vennemann (1975). Some of the examples of intonational boundary flagging I owe to Downing (1970); my general view of intonation in part to Bolinger (1958, 1972), in part to Trager and Smith (1951); some of the contrastive stress examples to George Lakoff (*John called Mary a Democrat,...*) and to Paul Schachter (*doctor in Los Angeles...*) (personal communications). My views have been modified in various ways by Peter Ladefoged (personal communications and in several publications) and by Schmerling (1972).

CHAPTER IV

The diagraming 'procedures' outlined here go back to structural linguistics as exemplified, for example, in Gleason (1955). The impression of some contemporary students that such tree-diagrams are novel devices belonging especially to the transformational tradition is mistaken [see, e.g., Nida (1943)].

CHAPTER V

The numerous rules referred to in Chapters V, VI, and VII are to be found all over the transformational literature. I do not know, in most cases, who first invented each one. A great many of them go back to Chomsky (1957), some to the first MIT linguistics dissertation [Lees (1960)], some to Katz and Postal (1964), some to Rosenbaum (1967). The richest source of information about Raising rules is Postal (1974), but there are no other comparable studies of the ramifications of a single rule. The cyclic principle of rule application is the classical position of Chomsky (1965); the theory of rule government was developed by Lakoff (1970*a*).

CHAPTER VI

The analysis of performatives is due to Ross (1970*b*), Austin (1962), and Searle (1969). The discussion of communication strategies such as 'incrementation' owes much to Talmy Givón (personal communications and forthcoming papers). The notion of 'tracer elements' is identical with the notion 'sentence trappings' in Langacker (1972), though independently conceived and characterized. Chomsky's 'trace theory' of conditions on transformations [in Anderson and Kiparsky (1973)] was unknown to me at the time this chapter was written, and that theory itself still remains obscure to me. The analysis of the comparative construction I owe to Bartsch and Vennemann (1972). Questions of ease of processing go back at least to the beginnings of transformational literature—e.g., Chomsky (1957). Notions of 'foregrounding' and such pragmatic considerations are due mainly to the work of the Czech formalists [see Vachek (1966)]. The idea of Conjunction-reduction as the source of relative clauses I owe to Thompson (1971); Conjunction-reduction goes back to Chomsky's earliest work. The rule of Gapping is due to Ross (1970*a*). Pronominalization was very insightfully studied by Langacker (1969), in particular the question of the governing relation to pronominal antecedents. The Yoruba and Finnish examples I owe to Keenan (forthcoming *b*), as well as the generalization they suggest about variation in the logical expressive power of languages.

CHAPTER VII

The analysis of imperative constructions, without a higher verb of command, dates from earliest transformational theory; the higher-verb analysis dates from Lakoff (1970*a*)—actually 1965 to most of the active workers in the field. My discussion of reflexives depends heavily on Keenan (1972). In the text I have acknowledged in particular my debt to Postal for the discussion of the phenomenon of Raising. The discussion of Infinitive-formation owes much to Kiparsky and Kiparsky (1970), and to Stockwell, Schachter, and Partee (1973). The discussion of Gerund-formation contains a claim about prepositional government that originates (to my knowledge) with Stockwell, Schachter, and Partee (1973—actually 1968 in its first-distributed form), but the claim was independently made by Newmeyer (1969). There are many cases of such convergence among scholars working in the same field. The issues separating the divergent lines of development within Chomskyan syntactic theory have been most clearly formulated by Seuren (1972) and Hawkins (1974).

Suggestions about Further Reading

Transformational grammarians have been exceptionally well-served by anthologists (including, of course, many of their own number), so that a large proportion of the better literature is readily available in just a few books. The first of these important collections was Fodor and Katz (1964), containing both republications and original papers (especially Klima on negation). A number of classic papers are reprinted in Reibel and Schane (1969) and in Jacobs and Rosenbaum (1970). The forthcoming volume òn transformational syntax edited by Arnold Zwicky in the Penguin Modern Linguistic Series should make available many of the more recent such papers.

The enormous impact that transformational theory made upon the academic linguistic community in less than ten years was due in part to the cohesiveness and doctrinal unity of the theory from 1955 to 1965. This is apparent in all the work of Chomsky through *Aspects* (1965), and it includes Lees (1960), Katz and Postal (1964), Klima (1964), and Rosenbaum (1967), the latter actually completed and widely circulated in 1965. The theory as developed up to that point is represented in pedagogical materials which leave the impression that we were but a few steps away from a final solution of most of the problems found in the syntax of natual languages—especially English. The beginner-oriented accounts of the unified theory include Jacobs and Rosenbaum (1968, 1971), Burt (1971), and Liles (1971). General introductory texts written during this same period, but more comprehensive, covering syntax as only one sub-area of linguistics, are Lyons (1968), Langacker (1967), and, best of all, Langacker (1972). The earliest of the introductory texts on transformational grammar, Bach (1964), remained without peer until Langacker (1972) and Grinder and Elgin (1973). Langendoen (1969) moves away from the earlier doctrinal types toward Grinder and Elgin. Langendoen (1970) is an appetizer, intended for secondary teachers of English who are mildly curious about the 'new' grammar. Bach (1974) is now the standard advanced introduction to transformational grammar. Had it been available when I was writing the present book, this one might well have been geared to it more effectively; but the two books are, on the whole, compatible and complementary. Appearing on the day that the final draft of this book was put in the mail to the publisher was Akmajian and Heny (1975), which takes an approach quite different from mine to the question of what is fundamental in syntax. It is a very thorough, step-by-step, formal development of a conservative version (i.e., closer to the earlier form) of transformational grammar known as the 'extended standard theory', the version favored by, e.g., Chomsky, Jackendoff, Emonds, and Bresnan, in opposition to the developments known as 'generative semantics' or 'semantic syntax'.

The earlier work, the 'classical' period of transformational theory, is discussed in relation to psychological and philosophical problems of the same period (early 1960's) by Lyons (1970). Shortly after 1965, there was an expansion of the world-view of most of the younger syntacticians (and many of the older ones) which sharply refocused the directions of research. Quite abruptly, most syntacticians of the transformationalist persuasion discovered that they had no notion where syntax ended and semantics began [see Bach (1971b)]. The questions posed first (within this general tradition) by Katz and Postal (1964)—a book which far from 'integrating' linguistic theory was the beginning of such sharply diverging viewpoints that there is no longer a single transformational theory but many theories which utilize the notion 'transformational rule' in some central way—initiated far-ranging work into the conditions on semantic interpretation. This new direction is to be seen in the anthologies of Bach and Harms (1968), wherein three of the four papers break sharply with the classical transformational model; of Bierwisch and Heidolph (1970); of Fillmore and Langendoen (1971); of Steinberg and Jakobovits (1971); and of Keenan (forthcoming *a*). Some of the central issues of this break between pre- and post-*Aspects* (1965) theories are aired by leading authorities in Peters (1972), and set forth pedagogically in Grinder and Elgin (1973) and Bach (1974).

On a track partially independent of but interacting with these developments in interesting ways is work on semantics and logical structure that is due mainly to the influence of logicians on syntacticians. This includes especially Bartsch and Vennemann (1972), Bartsch (1971, 1972), Keenan (forthcoming *b*), Lakoff (1970*b*, 1971), McCawley (1970*b*), Partee (1970), Sanders (1972), Seuren (1969, 1972, 1974), Vennemann (1973*a*, forthcoming *b*). For the beginner there is no very neat point of entry into these developments, but Keenan (1972) is a good starting place. A very advanced study of the logical representation of natural language is Bartsch (1972), in German (an English translation has been announced, to be available soon); at the other extreme, just as advanced from the syntactic end of the same spectrum, is Postal (1974). Sharing this general view of the primary role of semantics is Chafe (1970), but Chafe does not appear to have been influenced as much by formal logic, nor does he use it elaborately in his representations of meaning.

The study of Surface Structures has come to be elaborated from two relatively independent viewpoints: the universalist-historical one in Greenberg (1963*a*), Lehmann (1973), Vennemann (1973*b*, forthcoming *b*), Bach (1971*a*), Li (1975), Li and Thompson (1975); and the perceptual-cognitive one in Bever and Langendoen (1972), Bever (1970), and elsewhere in psycholinguistic studies [e.g., Deese (1970), Greene (1972), and Fodor, Bever, and Garrett (1974)]. Such Surface Structure studies are reminiscent of much that went on under the name 'structuralist syntax' before 1960 [see Householder (1972)].

While after 1965 a substantial group—including Postal, McCawley, Lakoff, Bach, Langendoen, Sanders, Koutsoudas, and Keenan in the vanguard—moved toward the logical representation of the meaning of sentences, another group, headed by Chomsky himself, opposed this view with great vigor; the publications of Jackendoff, Bresnan, and Emonds, along with those of Chomsky from 1970 onward, may be taken as representative. A book which incorporates both Fillmore (1968) and Chomsky (1970), along with a summation of much of the work of the 'classical' period, is Stockwell, Schachter, and Partee (1973), which was actually completed in 1968.

While the split over the manner in which conditions on adequacy of semantic interpretation should be met widened from 1965 onward, the study of conditions on well-formedness took a giant stride forward with Ross (1967), unfortunately never published in spite of its enormous importance and value to the profession (it has been widely circulated in mimeographed form). Other basic work in this domain includes Perlmutter (1970), Lakoff (1970a), and Postal (1971), the latter two dating from 1965–68.

These notes about further reading are narrow in the sense that they are restricted to the transformational tradition (by and large), certain alternatives (logical syntax, as in Bartsch), and just a hint at precursors [see especially Householder's introduction to Householder (1972)]. The bibliography is also restricted: (1) to references in the discussion above, to references in the acknowledgments, and to references in the text; and (2) to a few other items of value and importance, such as Derwing (1973), an interesting critique of transformational theory, although mostly of the phonological theory associated with it, Gruber (1967), a stimulating study of the formal content of the lexicon, Householder (1971), and Searle (1969).

References

*intermediate difficulty
**substantial difficulty
†collection of papers, either original or reprinted

*AKMAJIAN, Adrian, and Frank HENY. 1975. *An Introduction to the Principles of Transformational Syntax*. Cambridge, Mass.: MIT Press.
**†ANDERSON, Stephen R., and Paul KIPARSKY (eds.). 1973. *Studies in Honor of Morris Halle*. New York: Holt, Rinehart & Winston.
**AUSTIN, J. L. 1962. *How to Do Things with Words*. Cambridge, Mass.: Harvard University Press.
**BACH, Emmon. 1964. *An Introduction to Transformational Grammar*. New York: Holt, Rinehart & Winston.
*————. 1971*a*. "Questions." *Linguistic Inquiry* 2.153–66.
*————. 1971*b*. "Syntax since *Aspects*." In O'BRIEN (ed.), 1971.
*————. 1974. *Syntactic Theory*. New York: Holt, Rinehart & Winston.
**†————, and Robert T. HARMS (eds.). 1968. *Universals in Linguistic Theory*. New York: Holt, Rinehart & Winston.
**BARTSCH, Renate. 1971. "Zum Problem pseudo-logischer Notationen in der Generativen Semantik." *Beiträge zur Linguistik und Informations-Verarbeitung*, vol. 21.

**———. 1972. *Adverbialsemantik.* Frankfurt: Athenäum Verlag.

**———, and Theo VENNEMANN. 1972. *Semantic Structures.* Frankfurt: Athenäum Verlag.

**BEVER, Thomas G. 1970. "The cognitive basis of linguistic structure." In HAYES (ed.), 1970.

**———, and D. T. LANGENDOEN. 1972. "The interaction of speech perception and grammatical structure in the evolution of language." In STOCKWELL and MACAULAY (eds.), 1972.

**†BIERWISCH, Manfred, and Karl E. HEIDOLPH (eds.). 1970. *Progress in Linguistics.* The Hague: Mouton & Co.

*BOLINGER, Dwight L. 1952. "Linear modification." *Publications of the Modern Language Association of America* 67.1117–44.

**———. 1958. "A theory of pitch accent in English." *Word* 14.109–49.

*———. 1972. "Accent is predictable (if you're a mind-reader)." *Language* 48.633–44.

**BOTHA, R. P. 1968. *The Function of the Lexicon in Transformational Generative Grammar.* The Hague: Mouton & Co.

**BRESNAN, Joan. 1970. "On complementizers: towards a syntactic theory of complement types." *Foundations of Language* 6.297–321.

**BULL, William E. 1960. *Time, Tense, and the Verb.* Berkeley & Los Angeles: University of California Press.

BURT, Marina K. 1971. *From Deep to Surface Structure: An Introduction to Transformational Syntax.* New York: Harper & Row.

**CHAFE, Wallace L. 1970. *Meaning and the Structure of Language.* Chicago: University of Chicago Press.

*CHOMSKY, Noam. 1957. *Syntactic Structures.* The Hague: Mouton & Co.

**———. 1965. *Aspects of the Theory of Syntax.* Cambridge, Mass.: MIT Press.

———. 1967. "The general properties of language." In DARLEY (ed.), 1967.

**———. 1970. "Remarks on nominalization." In JACOBS and ROSENBAUM (eds.), 1970.

**———. 1971. "Deep structure, surface structure, and semantic interpretation." In STEINBERG and JAKOBOVITS (eds.), 1971.

**———. 1972. "Some empirical issues in the theory of transformational grammar." In PETERS (ed.), 1972.

**———. 1973. "Conditions on transformations." In ANDERSON and KIPARSKY (eds.), 1973.

**†DARLEY, F. L. (ed.). 1967. *Brain Mechanisms Underlying Speech and Language.* New York and London: Grune & Stratton.

**†DAVIDSON, D., and G. HARMAN (eds.). 1972. *Semantics of Natural Language.* Dordrecht: D. Reidel.

DEESE, James. 1970. *Psycholinguistics.* Boston: Allyn & Bacon.

**DERWING, Bruce L. 1973. *Transformational Grammar as a Theory of Language Acquisition.* Cambridge, Eng.: Cambridge University Press.

**†DINGWALL, William Orr. 1971. *A Survey of Linguistic Science.* College Park, Md.: Linguistics Program, University of Maryland.

**DOWNING, Bruce. 1970. "Syntactic structure and phonological phrasing in English." University of Texas dissertation.

**EMONDS, Joseph E. 1970. "Root and structure-preserving transformations." MIT dissertation. [Revised version, Academic Press, 1975.]

*FILLMORE, Charles. 1966. "A proposal concerning English prepositions." *Report of the 17th Annual Round Table Meeting.* Washington, D.C.:

Georgetown University Press. [Revised version in REIBEL and SCHANE (eds.), 1969.]

*———. 1968. "The case for case." In BACH and HARMS (eds.), 1968.

**†———, and D. T. LANGENDOEN (eds.). 1971. *Studies in Linguistic Semantics.* New York: Holt, Rinehart & Winston.

*FODOR, J. A., T. G. BEVER, and M. F. GARRETT. 1974. *The Psychology of Language.* New York: McGraw-Hill.

*†———, and Jerrold J. KATZ (eds.). 1964. *The Structure of Languages.* Englewood Cliffs, N.J.: Prentice-Hall.

*FRASER, Bruce J. 1965. "An examination of the verb–particle construction in English." MIT dissertation.

**†GARVIN, Paul (ed.). 1970. *Cognition: A Multiple View.* New York: Spartan Books.

**GIVÓN, Talmy. Forthcoming. "Toward a discourse definition of syntax."

GLEASON, H. A. 1955. *An Introduction to Descriptive Linguistics.* New York: Holt, Rinehart & Winston.

*GREENBERG, Joseph H. 1963*a.* "Some universals of grammar with particular reference to the order of meaningful elements." In GREENBERG (ed.), 1963*b.*

*†——— (ed.). 1963*b. Universals of Language.* Cambridge, Mass.: MIT Press. [Revised, 2nd edition, 1966.]

GREENE, Judith. 1972. *Psycholinguistics: Chomsky and Psychology.* Harmondsworth, Eng.: Penguin.

*GRINDER, John. 1972. "On the cycle in syntax." In KIMBALL (ed.), 1972.

———, and Suzette Haden ELGIN. 1973. *Guide to Transformational Grammar.* New York: Holt, Rinehart & Winston.

**GRUBER, Jeffrey. 1967. *Functions of the Lexicon in Formal Descriptive Grammar.* Santa Monica, Calif.: Systems Development Corp.

**HALLIDAY, M. A. K. 1961. "Categories of the theory of grammar." *Word* 17.241–92.

**HARRIS, Zellig S. 1952. "Discourse analysis." *Language* 28.1–30.

**———. 1957. "Co-occurrence and transformation in linguistic structure." *Language* 33.283–340. [Reprinted in FODOR and KATZ (eds.), 1964.]

**HAWKINS, J. A. 1974. "Definiteness and indefiniteness." Cambridge University dissertation.

*†HAYES, J. (ed.). 1970. *Cognition and the Development of Language.* New York: John Wiley & Sons.

**HETZRON, Robert. 1971. "The deep structure of the statement." *Linguistics* 65.25–63 (Jan. 1971).

**———. 1973. "Surfacing." *Studi Italiani di Linguistica Teorica ed Applicada* 2, 1–2.

**———. 1974. "A synthetical-generative approach to language." *Linguistics* 138.29–62 (Oct. 15, 1974).

*HILL, Archibald A. 1961. "Grammaticality." *Word* 17.1–10.

*HOCKETT, Charles. 1968. *The State of the Art.* The Hague: Mouton & Co.

*HOUSEHOLDER, Fred W. 1971. *Linguistic Speculations.* Cambridge, Eng.: Cambridge University Press.

*†———. 1972. "Introduction." *Syntactic Theory I: Structuralist.* Harmondsworth, Eng.: Penguin.

*HUDSON, Grover. 1972. "Is deep structure linear?" *UCLA Papers in Syntax* 2. Los Angeles, Calif.

**HUTCHINS, W. J. 1971. *The Generation of Syntactic Structures from a Semantic Base.* Amsterdam: North-Holland Publishing Co.

**JACKENDOFF, Ray. 1972. *Semantic Interpretation in Generative Grammar.* Cambridge, Mass.: MIT Press.

JACOBS, Roderick A., and Peter S. ROSENBAUM. 1968. *English Transformational Grammar.* Waltham, Mass.: Ginn & Co.

†———— (eds.). 1970. *Readings in English Transformational Grammar.* Waltham, Mass.: Ginn & Co.

†————. 1971. *Transformations, Style, and Meaning.* Waltham, Mass.: Xerox.

*KATZ, Jerrold J., and Paul M. POSTAL. 1964. *An Integrated Theory of Linguistic Descriptions.* Cambridge, Mass.: MIT Press.

**KEENAN, Edward. 1972. "On semantically based grammar." *Linguistic Inquiry* 3.413–61.

**†———— (ed.). Forthcoming *a. Formal Semantics of Natural Language. Proceedings of the 1973 Conference on Formal Semantics of Natural Language.* Cambridge, Eng.: Cambridge University Press.

**————. Forthcoming *b.* "Logical expressive power and syntactic variation in natural languages." In KEENAN (ed.), forthcoming *a.*

**†KIMBALL, John (ed.). 1972. *Syntax and Semantics, Vol. I.* New York: Seminar Press.

**————. 1973*a. The Formal Theory of Grammar.* Englewoods Cliffs, N.J.: Prentice-Hall.

**†———— (ed.). 1973*b. Syntax and Semantics, Vol. II.* New York: Seminar Press.

*KING, H. V. 1970. "On blocking the rules for contraction in English." *Linguistic Inquiry* 2.134–6.

*KIPARSKY, Paul, and Carol KIPARSKY. 1970. "Fact." In BIERWISCH and HEIDOLPH (eds.), 1970.

**KLIMA, Edward S. 1964. "Negation in English." In FODOR and KATZ (eds.), 1964.

*LAKOFF, George. 1968. "Instrumental adverbs and the concept of Deep Structure." *Foundations of Language* 4.4–29.

**————. 1970*a. Irregularity in Syntax.* New York: Holt, Rinehart & Winston.

**————. 1970*b.* "Linguistics and natural logic." *Synthese* 22, 1–2. [Reprinted in DAVIDSON and HARMAN (eds.), 1972.]

*————. 1970*c.* "Pronominalization, negation, and the analysis of adverbs." In JACOBS and ROSENBAUM (eds.), 1970.

*————. 1971. "Presupposition and relative well-formedness." In STEINBERG and JAKOBOVITS (eds.), 1971.

LANGACKER, Ronald. 1967. *Language and its Structure: Some Fundamental Linguistic Concepts.* New York: Harcourt, Brace, Jovanovich.

**————. 1969. "On pronominalization and the chain of command." In REIBEL and SCHANE (eds.), 1969.

————. 1972. *Fundamentals of Linguistic Analysis.* New York: Harcourt, Brace, Jovanovich.

LANGENDOEN, D. T. 1969. *The Study of Syntax: The Generative-Transformational Approach to the Structure of American English.* New York: Holt, Rinehart & Winston.

————. 1970. *Essentials of English Grammar.* New York: Holt, Rinehart & Winston.

**LEES, R. B. 1960. *The Grammar of English Nominalizations.* The Hague: Mouton & Co.

*————, and E. S. KLIMA. 1963. "Rules for English pronominalization." *Language* 39.17–28.

**LEHMANN, Winfred P. 1973. "A structural principle of language and its implications." *Language* 49.47–66.

**———. 1974. *Proto-Indo-European Syntax.* Austin: University of Texas Press.

**†LI, Charles N. (ed.). 1975. *Word Order and Word Order Change.* Austin: University of Texas Press.

*———, and Sandra A. THOMPSON. 1975. "The issue of word order in a synchronic grammar." In LI 1975.

LILES, Bruce L. 1971. *An Introductory Transformational Grammar.* Englewood Cliffs, N.J.: Prentice-Hall.

*LYONS, John. 1968. *Introduction to Theoretical Linguistics.* Cambridge, Eng.: Cambridge University Press.

———. 1970. *Noam Chomsky.* New York: Viking Press.

**McCAWLEY, James. 1968. "The role of semantics in a grammar." In BACH and HARMS (eds.), 1968.

**———. 1970a. "Semantic representation." In GARVIN (ed.), 1970.

**———. 1970b. "A program for logic." In DAVIDSON and HARMAN (eds.), 1972.

**———. 1970c. "English as a VSO language." *Language* 46.286–99.

**MONTAGUE, Richard. 1970. "English as a formal language." In B. VISENTINI (ed.), *Linguaggi nella societa a nella tecnica,* Milano, Italy.

*NEWMEYER, F. J. 1969. "The derivation of English action nominalizations." *Chicago Linguistic Society* 6.408–15.

*NIDA, E. A. 1943. "A synopsis of English syntax." University of Michigan dissertation. [2nd edition, revised, published by Mouton & Co., 1966.]

*NILSEN, Don Lee Fred. 1970. *Toward a Semantic Specification of Deep Case.* The Hague: Mouton & Co.

†O'BRIEN, R. J. (ed.). 1971. *Report of the Twenty-Second Annual Round Table Meeting on Linguistics and Language Studies, Monograph Series on Languages and Linguistics* 24. Washington, D.C.: Georgetown University Press.

**PARTEE, Barbara Hall. 1970. "Negation, conjunction, and quantifiers: syntax vs. semantics." *Foundations of Language* 6.153–65.

*———. 1971a. "On the requirement that transformations preserve meaning." In FILLMORE and LANGENDOEN (eds.), 1971.

**———. 1971b. "Linguistic metatheory." In DINGWALL (ed.), 1971.

**PERLMUTTER, David M. 1970. *Deep and Surface Structure Constraints in Syntax.* New York: Holt, Rinehart & Winston.

**†PETERS, Paul Stanley (ed.). 1972. *Goals of Linguistic Theory.* Englewood Cliffs, N.J.: Prentice-Hall.

*POPE, Emily. 1971. "Answers to Yes-No questions." *Linguistic Inquiry* 2.69–82.

POSTAL, Paul. 1964. "Underlying and superficial linguistic structure." *Harvard Educational Review* 34.246–66. [Reprinted in REIBEL and SCHANE (eds.), 1969.]

*———. 1970. "The method of universal grammar ." In GARVIN (ed.), 1970.

**———. 1971. *Cross-Over Phenomena.* New York: Holt, Rinehart & Winston.

**———. 1974. *On Raising.* Cambridge, Mass.: MIT Press.

*†REIBEL, David A., and Sanford A. SCHANE (eds.). 1969. *Modern Studies in English.* Englewood Cliffs, N.J.: Prentice-Hall.

**ROSENBAUM, Peter S. 1967. *The Grammar of English Predicate Complement Constructions.* Cambridge, Mass.: MIT Press.

**Ross, John R. 1967. "Constraints on variables in syntax." MIT dissertation.

**———. 1969. "The cyclic nature of English pronominalization." In Reibel and Schane (eds.), 1969.

**———. 1970a. "Gapping and the order of constituents." In Bierwisch and Heidolph (eds.), 1970.

*———. 1970b. "On declarative sentences." In Jacobs and Rosenbaum (eds.), 1970.

**Sanders, Gerald A. 1972. *Equational Grammar.* The Hague: Mouton & Co.

*Schachter, Paul. 1973. "Focus and relativization." *Language* 49.19–46.

**———, and Fe T. Otanes. 1972. *Tagalog Reference Grammar.* Berkeley & Los Angeles: University of California Press.

*Schmerling, Susan Fred. 1972. "Aspects of English sentence stress." University of Illinois dissertation. [Forthcoming, University of Texas Press, 1976.]

**Searle, John. 1969. *Speech Acts: An Essay in the Philosophy of Language.* Cambridge, Eng.: Cambridge University Press.

**Seuren, P. A. M. 1969. *Operators and Nucleus.* Cambridge, Eng.: Cambridge University Press.

**———. 1972. "Autonomous versus semantic syntax." *Foundations of Language* 8.237–65.

**———. 1974. *Semantic Syntax.* Oxford: Oxford University Press.

**†Steinberg, D., and L. Jakobovits (eds.). 1971. *Semantics: An Interdisciplinary Reader in Philosophy, Linguistics, Anthropology and Psychology.* Cambridge, Eng.: Cambridge University Press.

**†Stockwell, Robert P., and Ronald K. S. Macaulay (eds.). 1972. *Linguistic Change and Generative Theory.* Bloomington: Indiana University Press.

*Stockwell, R. P., Paul Schachter, and Barbara Hall Partee. 1973. *The Major Syntactic Structures of English.* New York: Holt, Rinehart & Winston.

*Thompson, Sandra A. 1971. "The deep structure of relative clauses." In Fillmore and Langendoen (eds.), 1971.

*———. 1973. "On subjectless gerunds in English." *Foundations of Language* 9.374–83.

**Trager, George L., and Henry Lee Smith, Jr. 1951. *An Outline of English Structure.* Norman, Okla.: Battenburg Press.

**Vachek, J. 1966. *The Linguistic School of Prague.* Bloomington, Ind.: Indiana University Press.

**Vennemann, Theo. 1973a. "Explanation in syntax." In Kimball (ed.), 1973b.

**———. 1973b. "Language type and word order." *Proceedings of 1973 Symposium on Typology, Prague.*

**———. 1975. "An explanation of 'drift'." In Li 1975.

**———. Forthcoming a. "Extraciation as a mechanism of word order change." [Paper read at UCLA, Spring 1974.]

**———. Forthcoming b. "Topics, sentence accent, ellipsis: a proposal for their formal treatment." In Keenan (ed.), forthcoming.

*Wall, Robert. 1972. *Introduction to Mathematical Linguistics.* Englewood Cliffs, N.J.: Prentice-Hall.

Index

Frequently-used linguistic terms are indexed only in their more important occurrences.